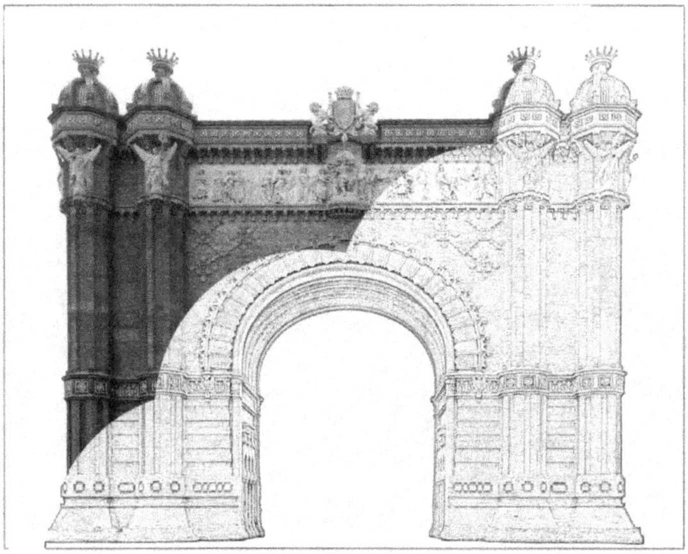

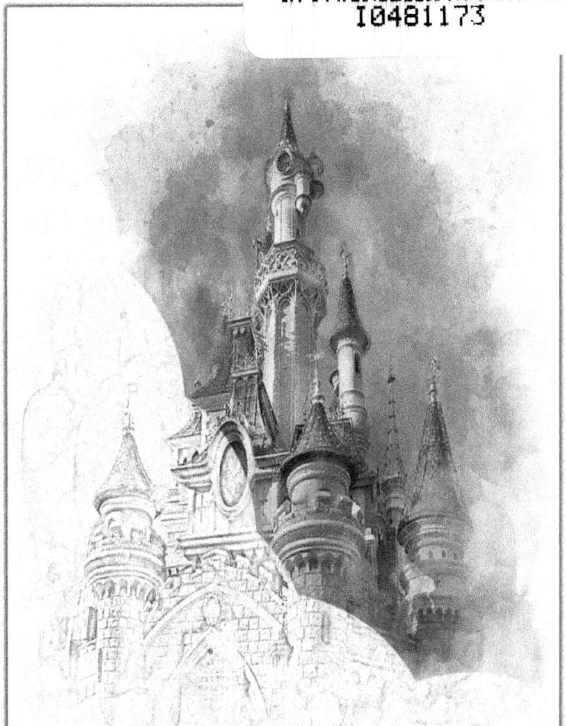

Architectural Beauty

Adult Coloring Book

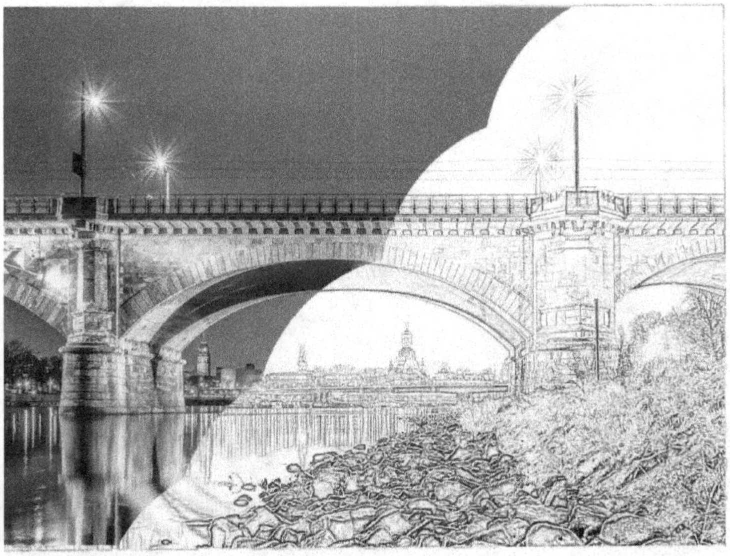

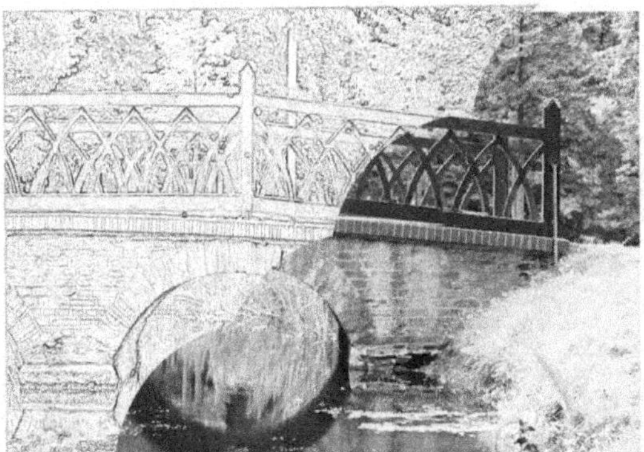

ISBN-13:
978-1983825705

ISBN-10:
1983825700

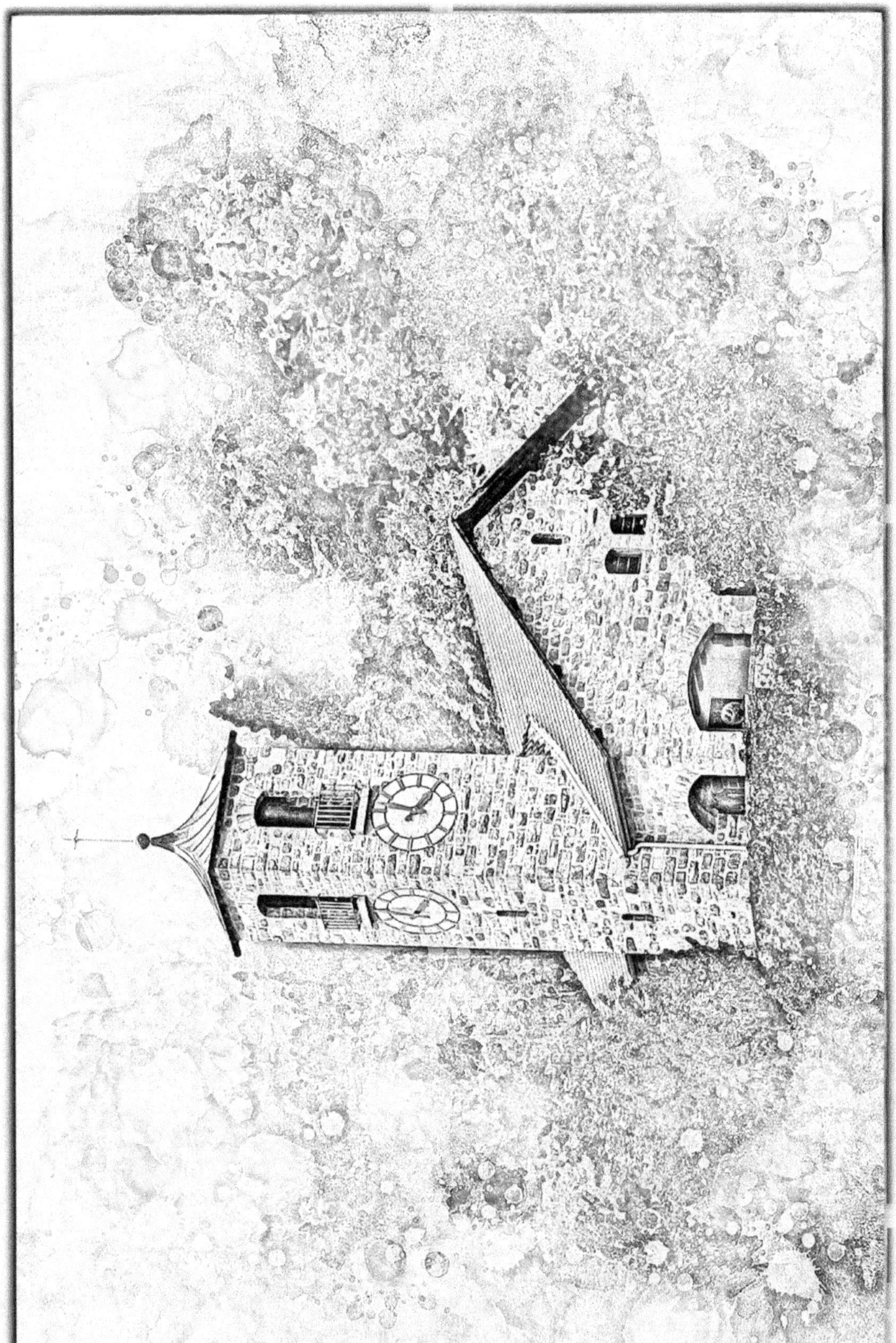

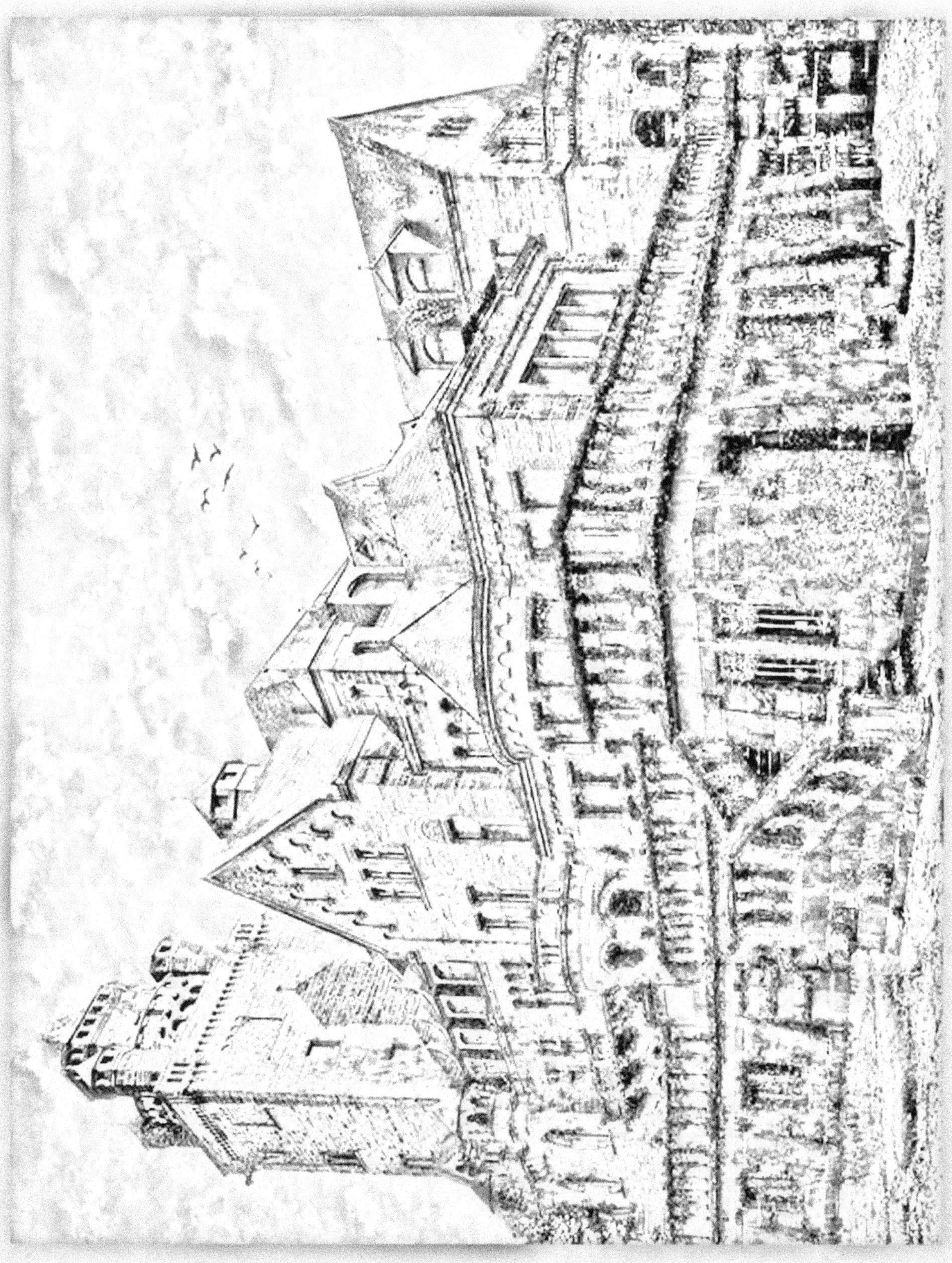

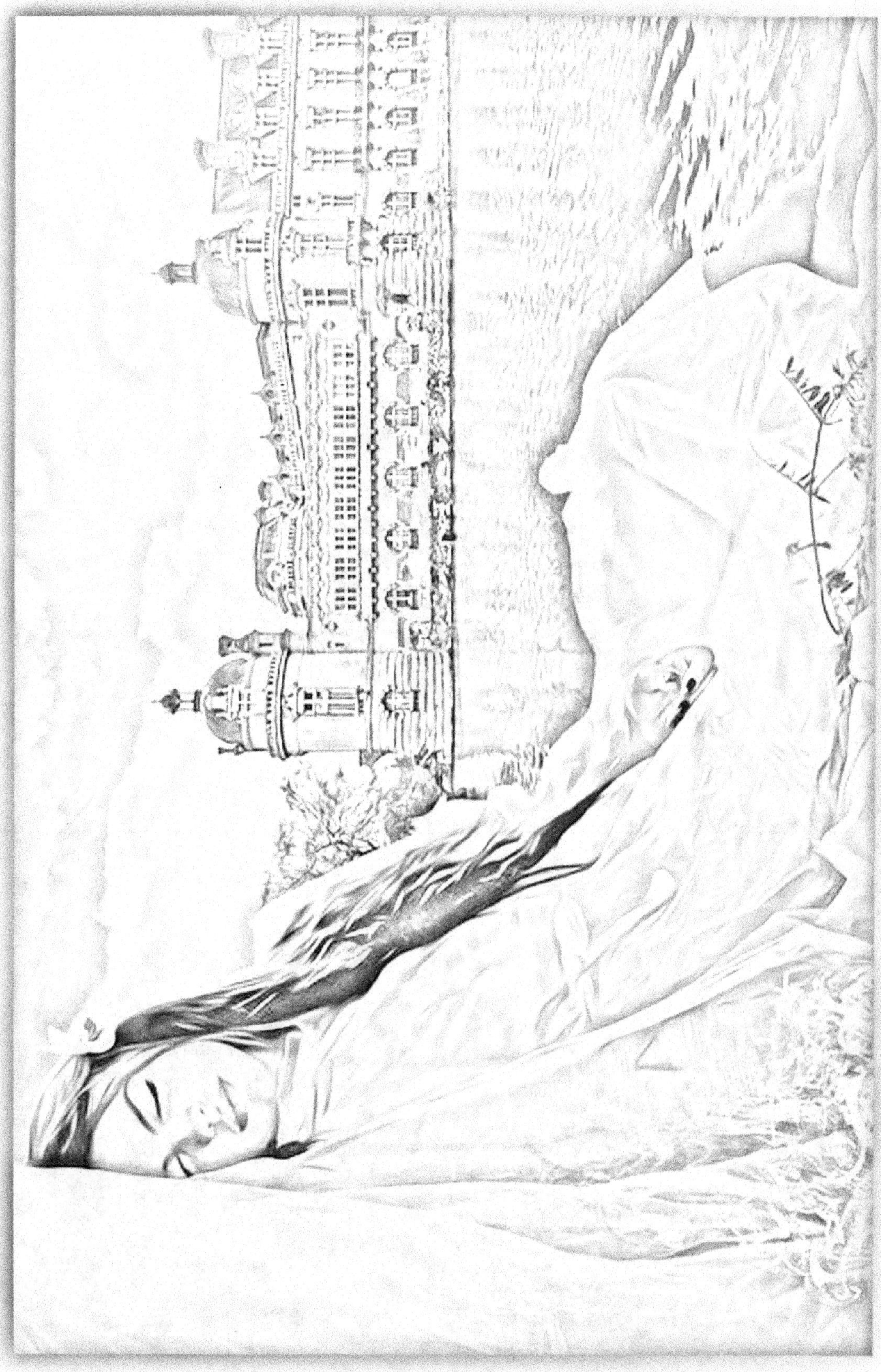

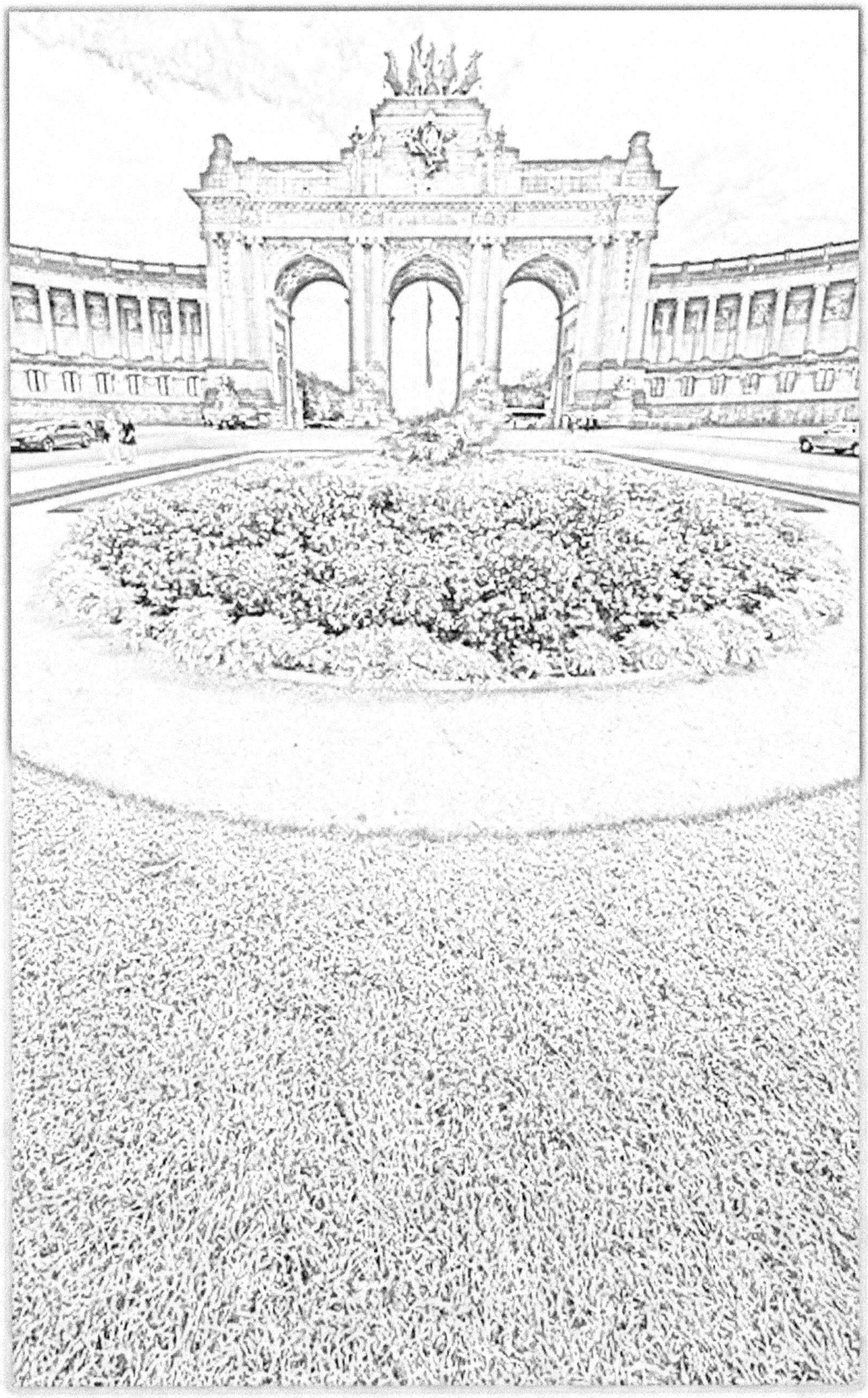

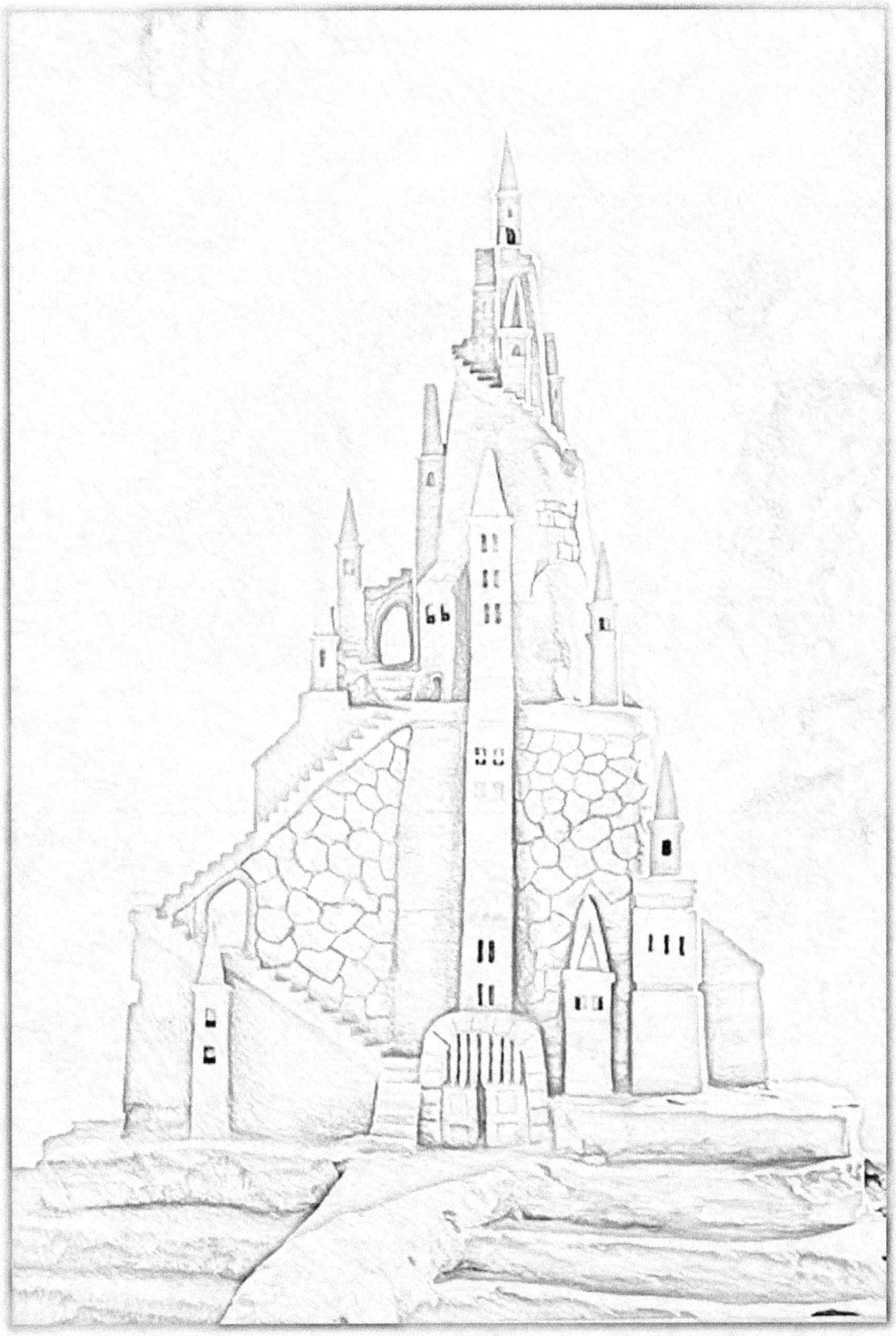

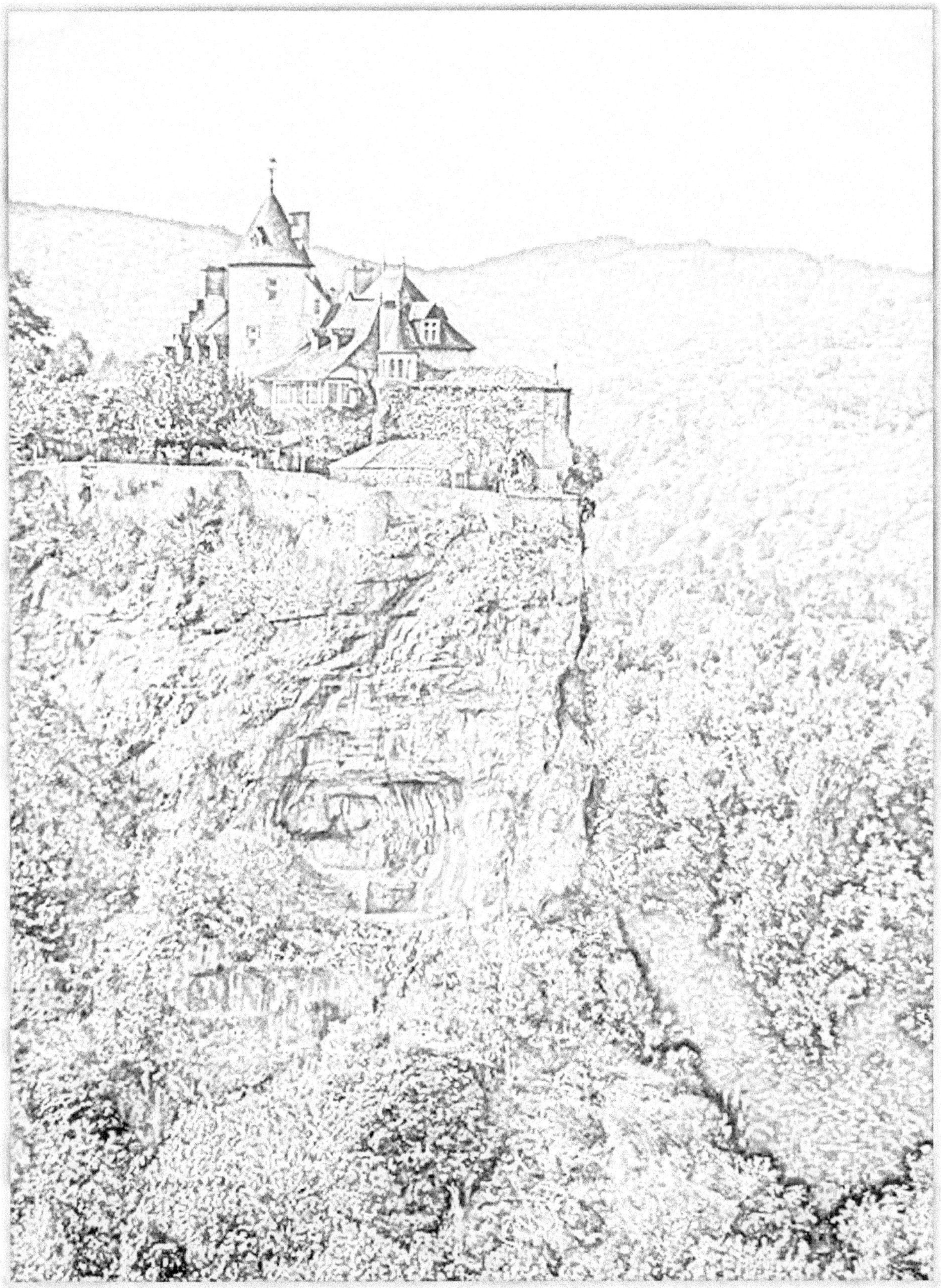

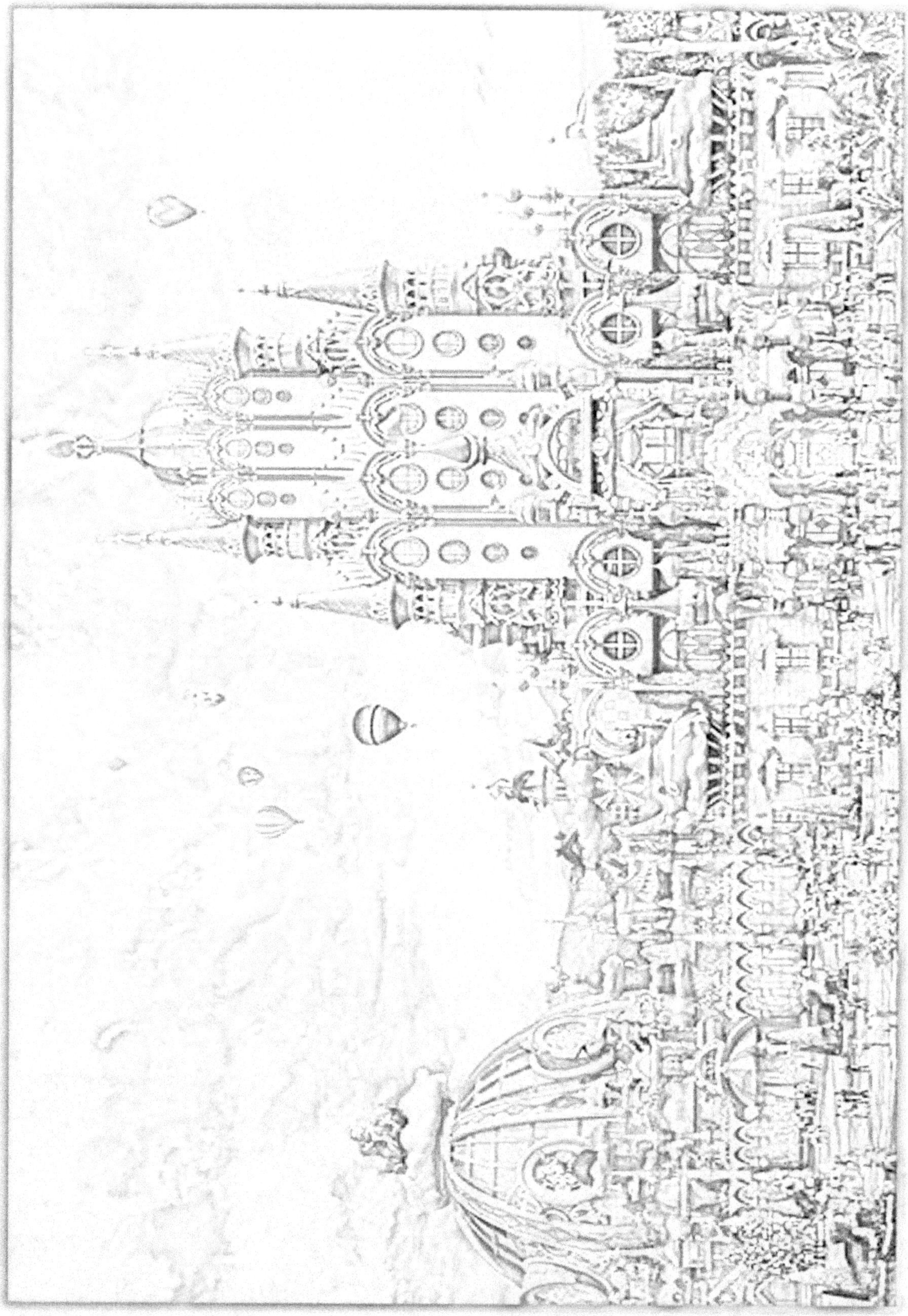

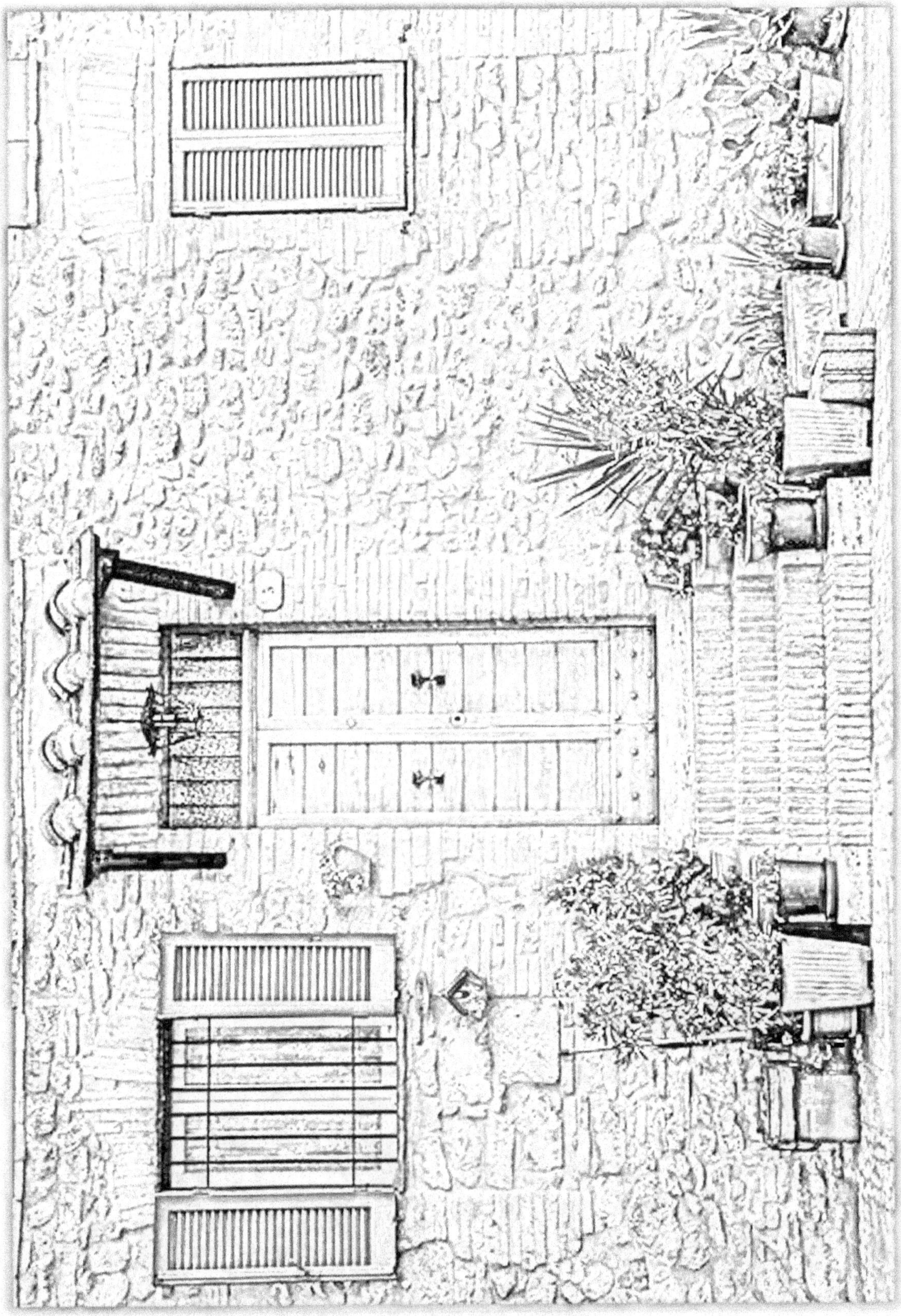

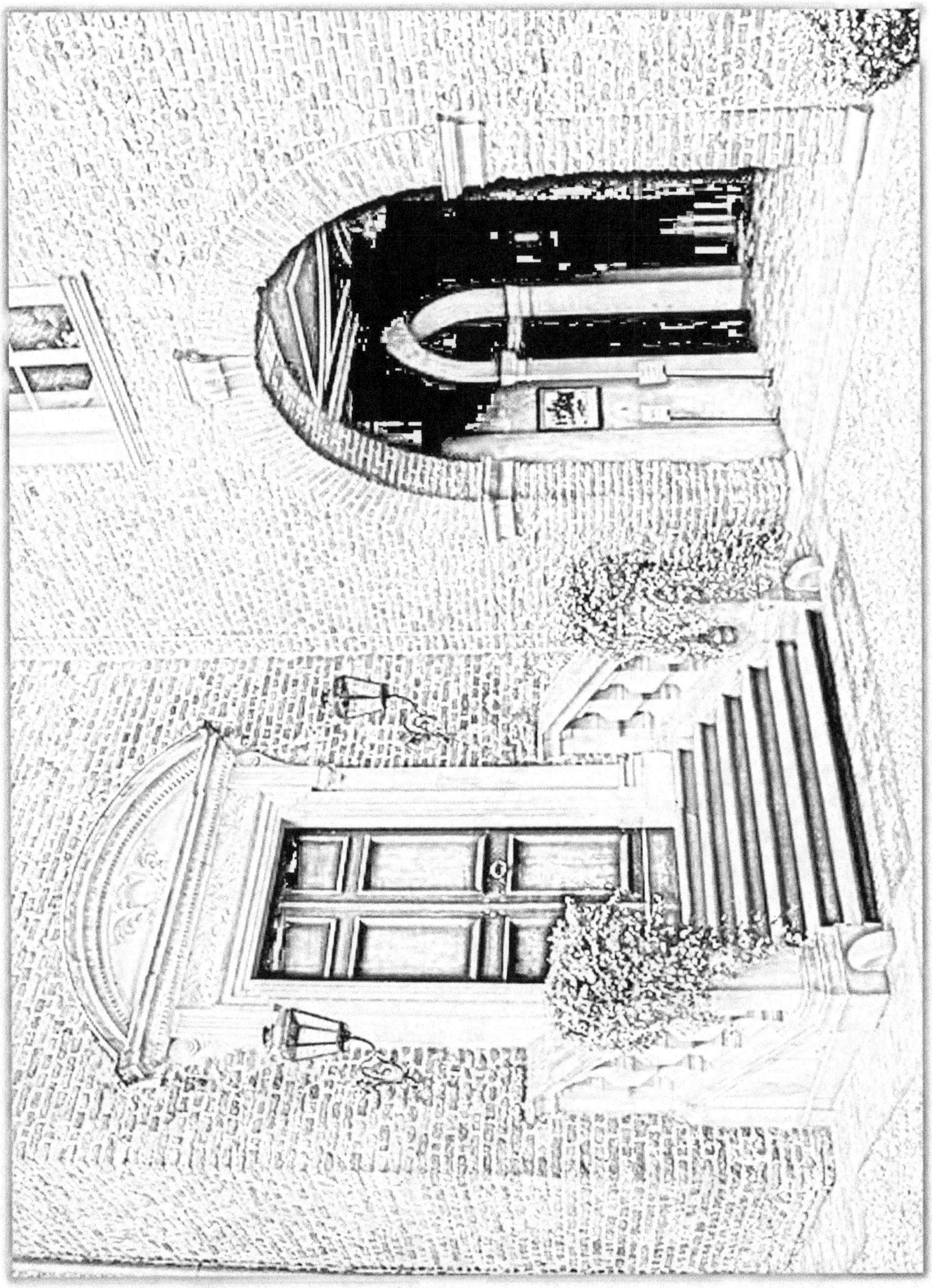

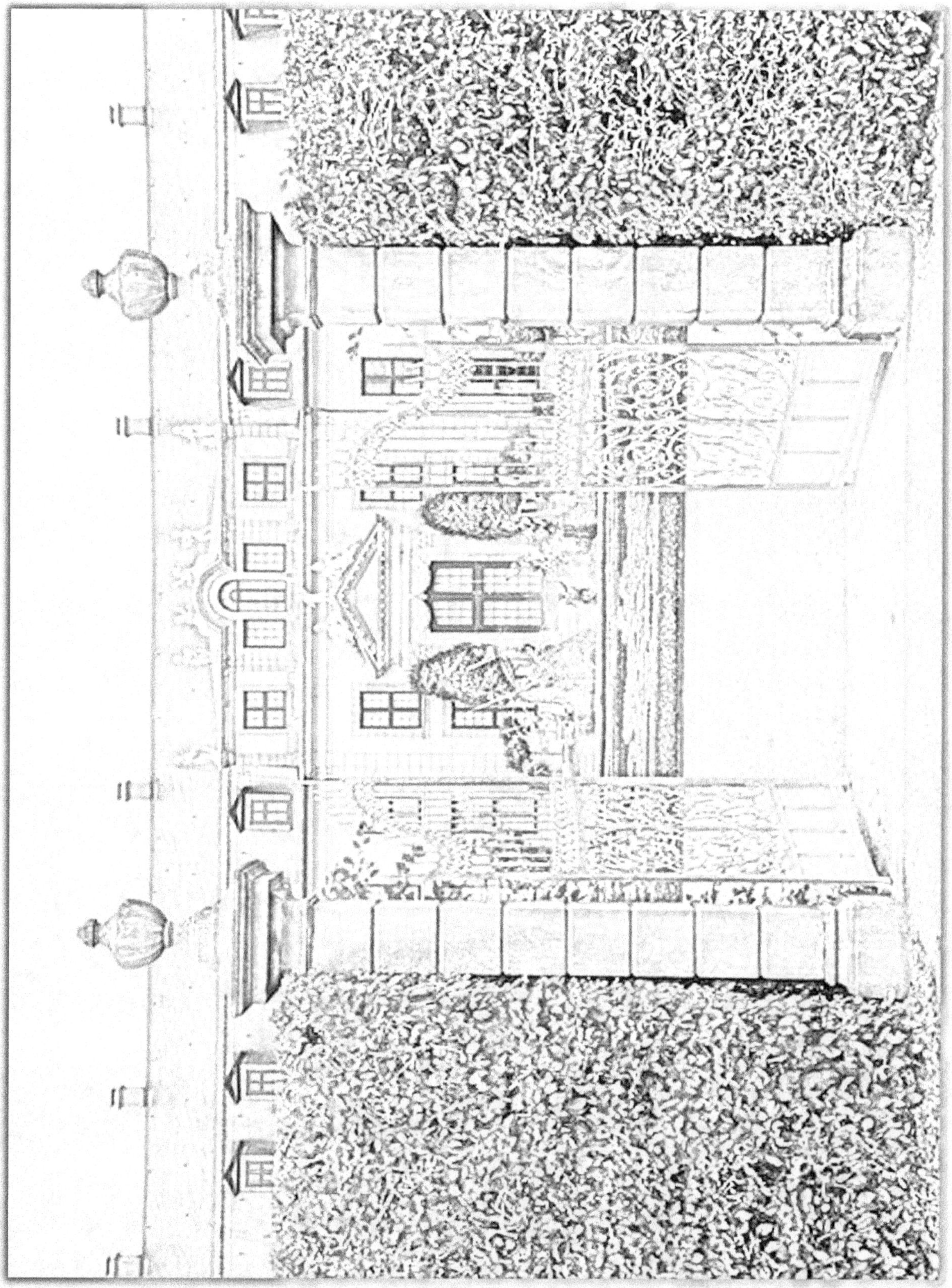

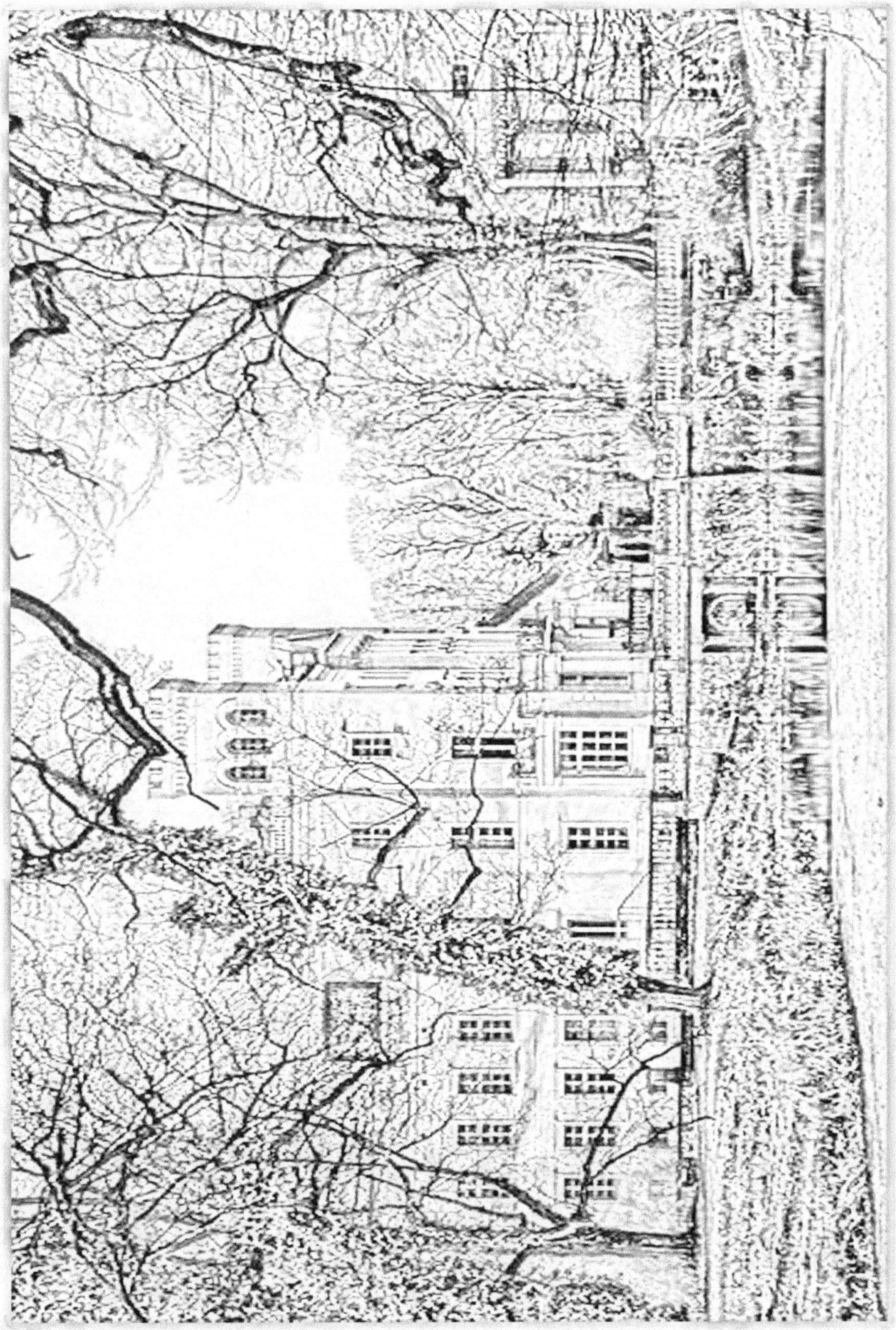

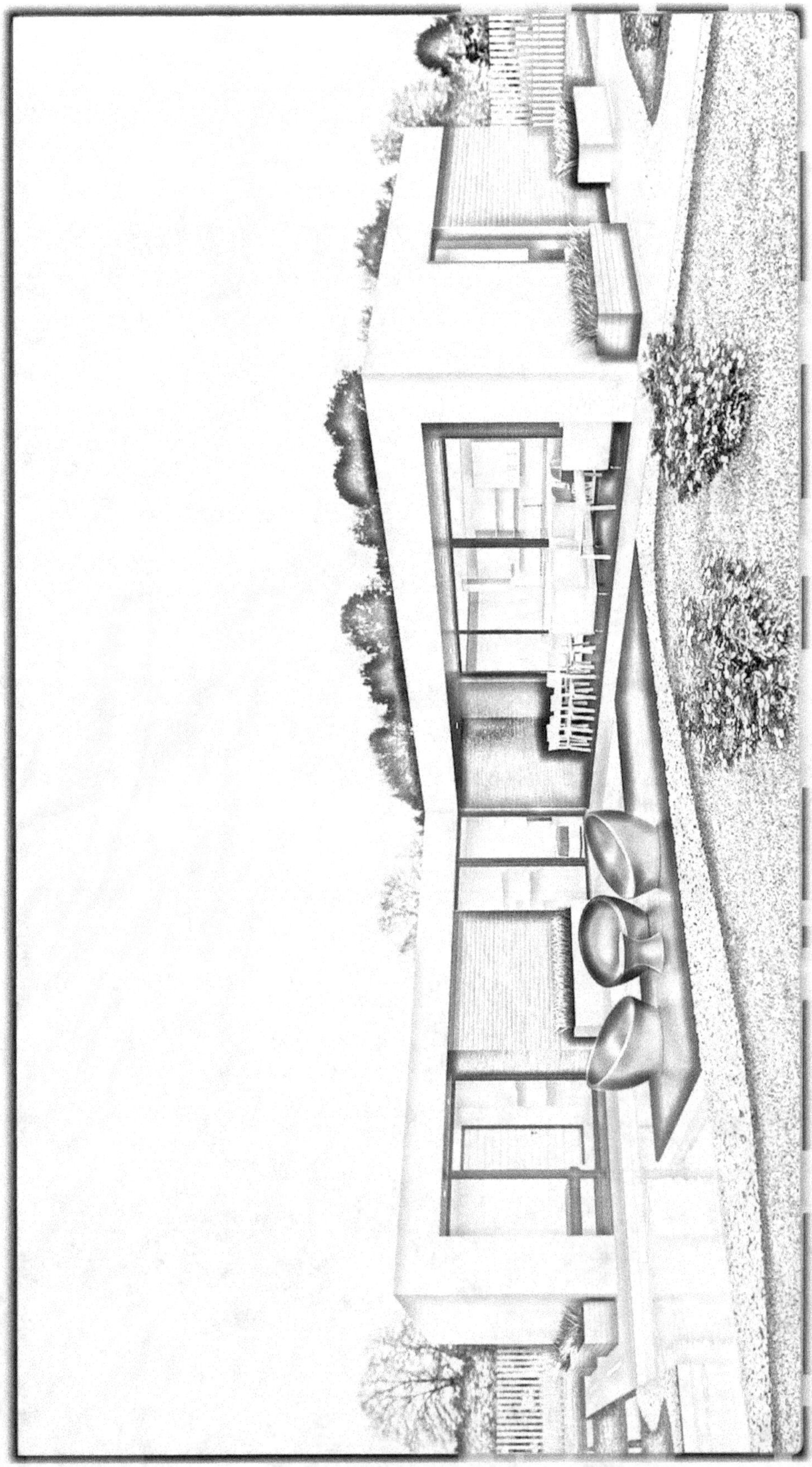

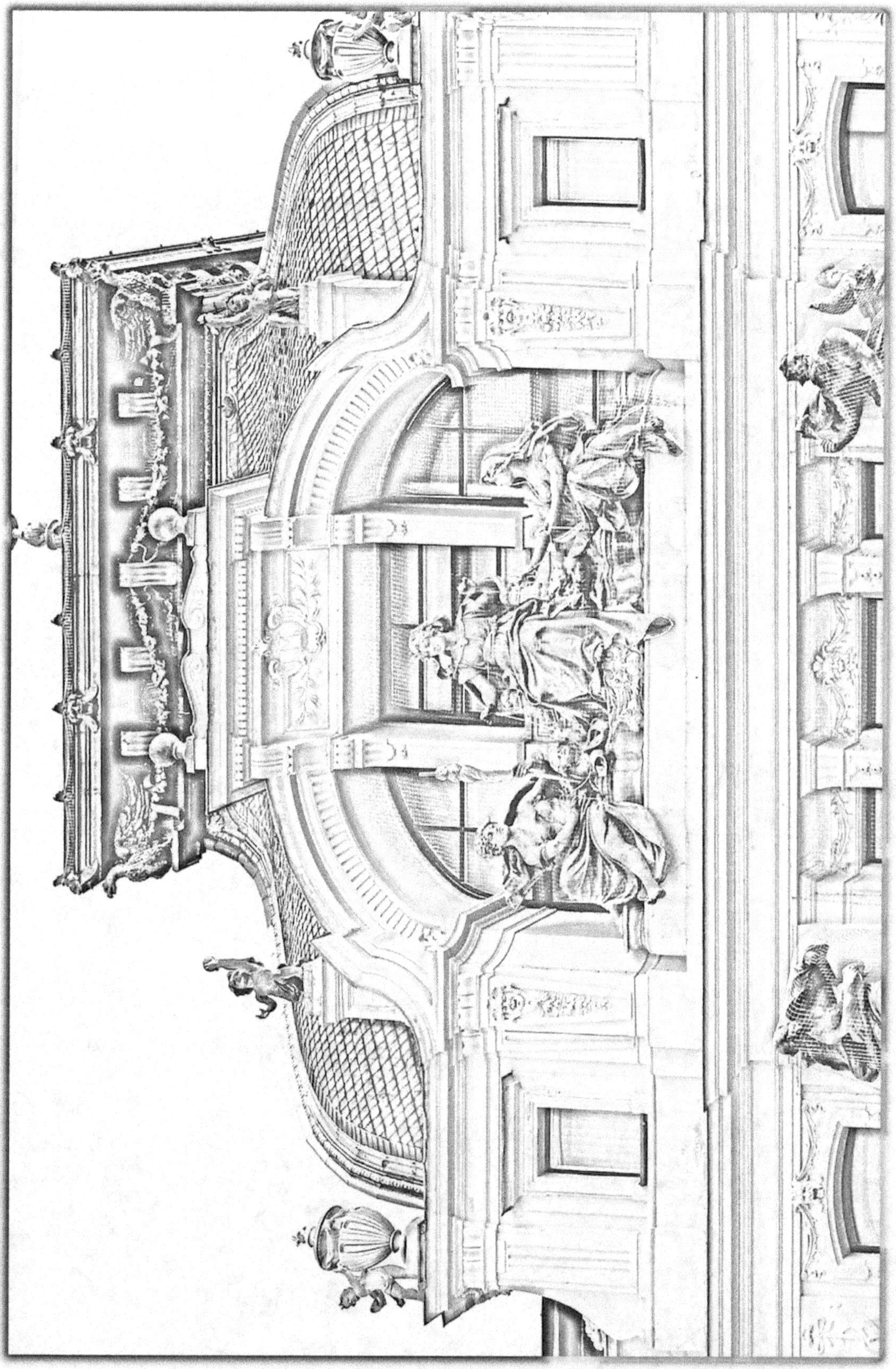

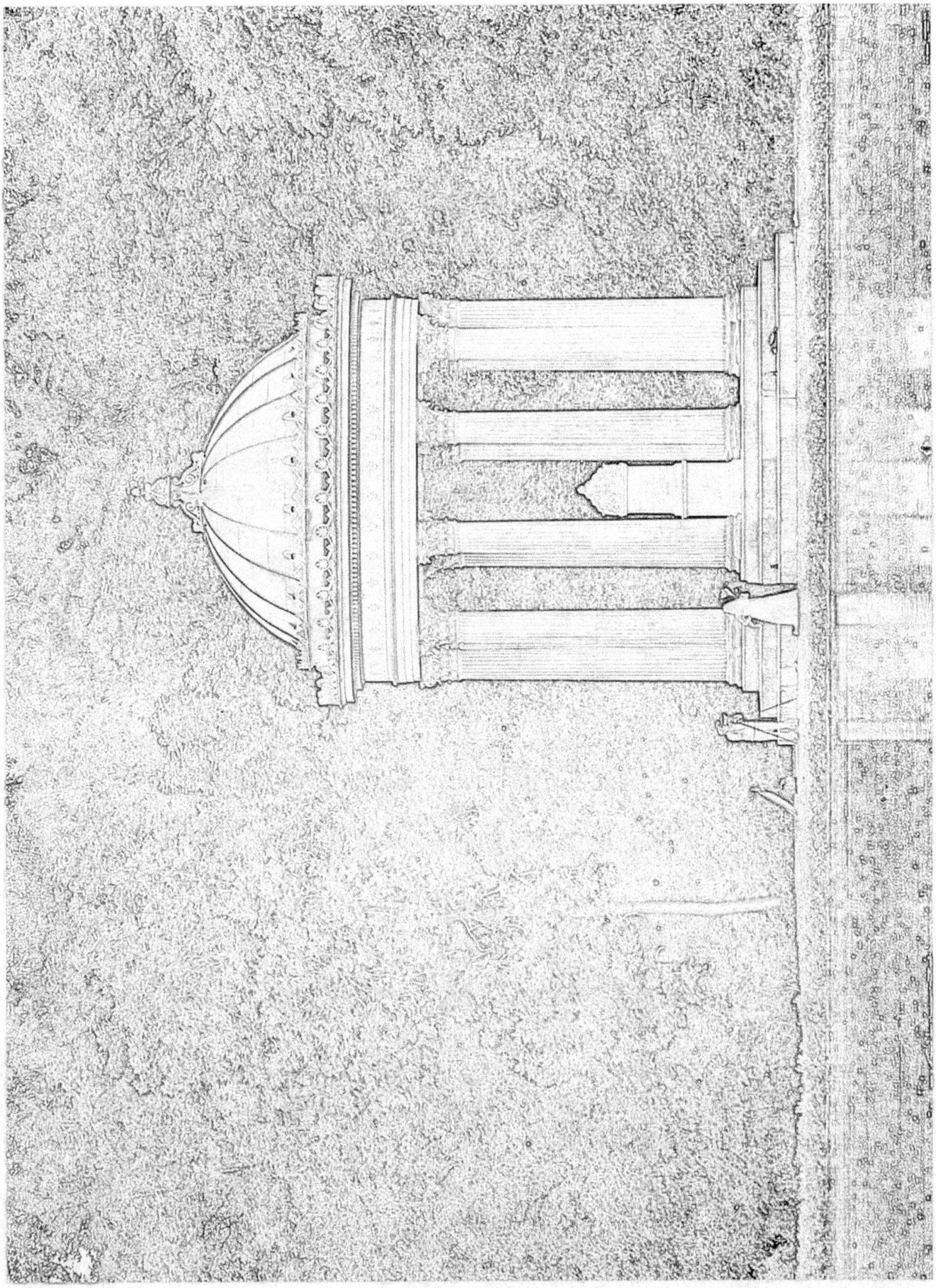

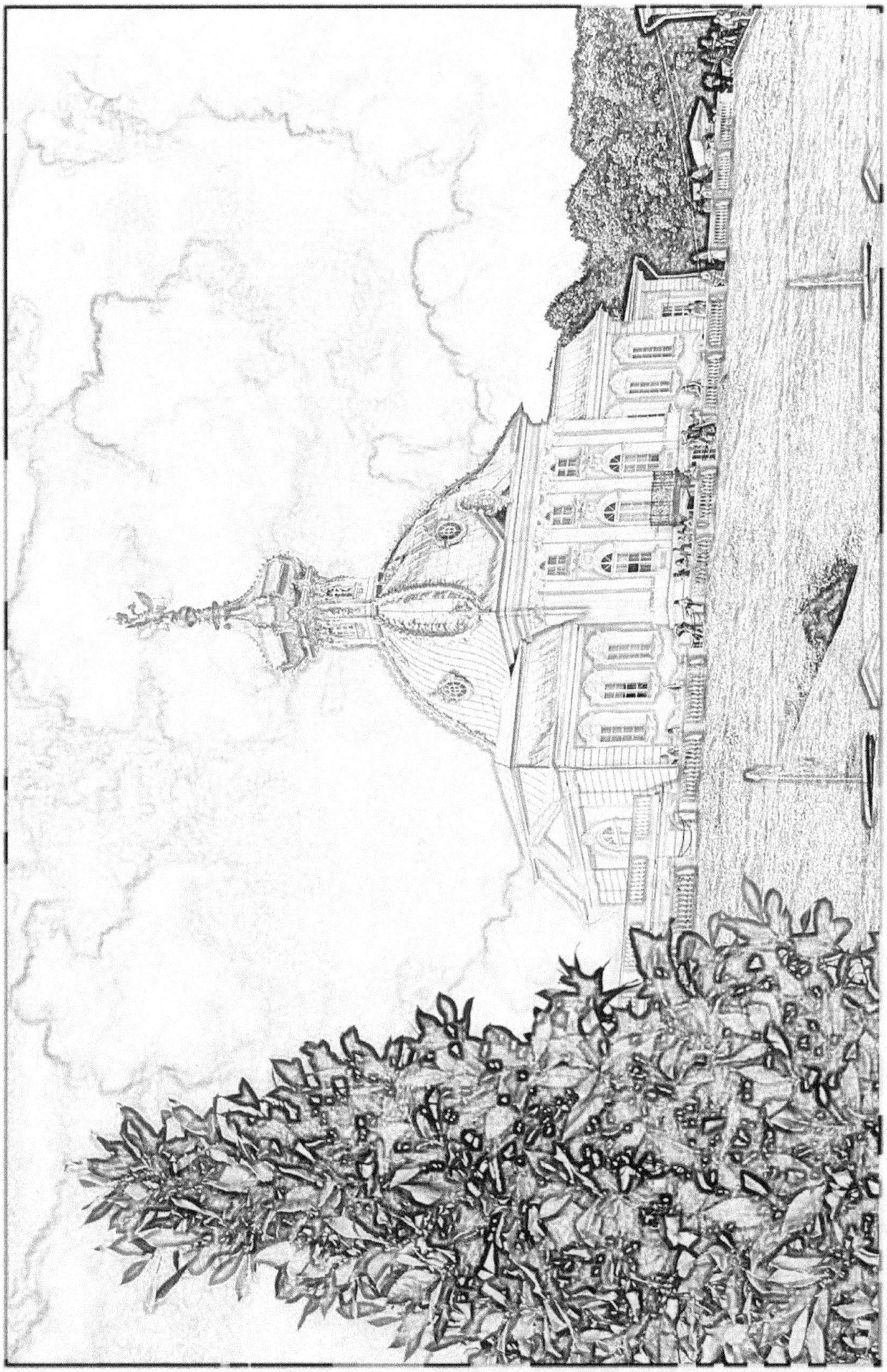

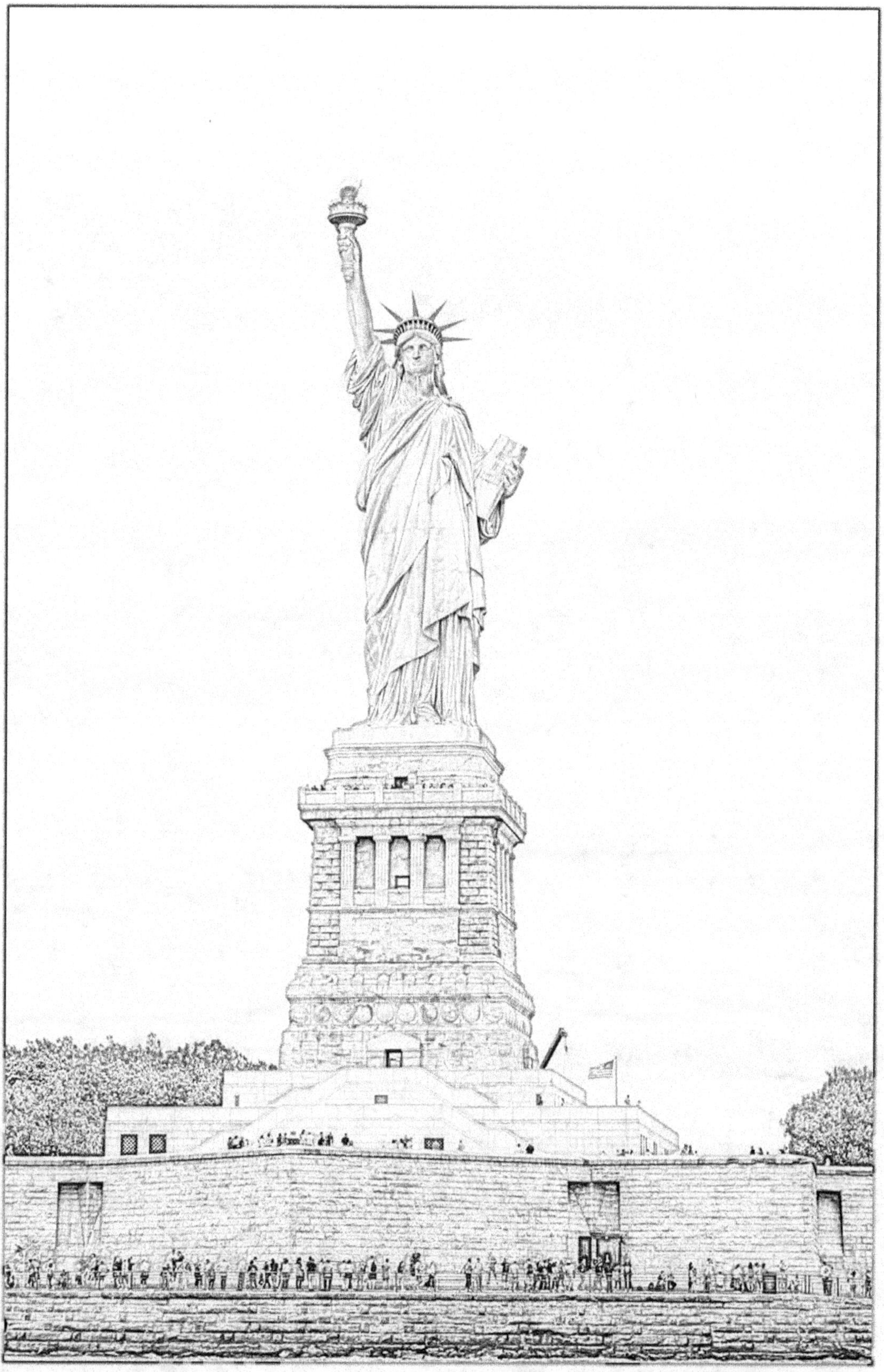

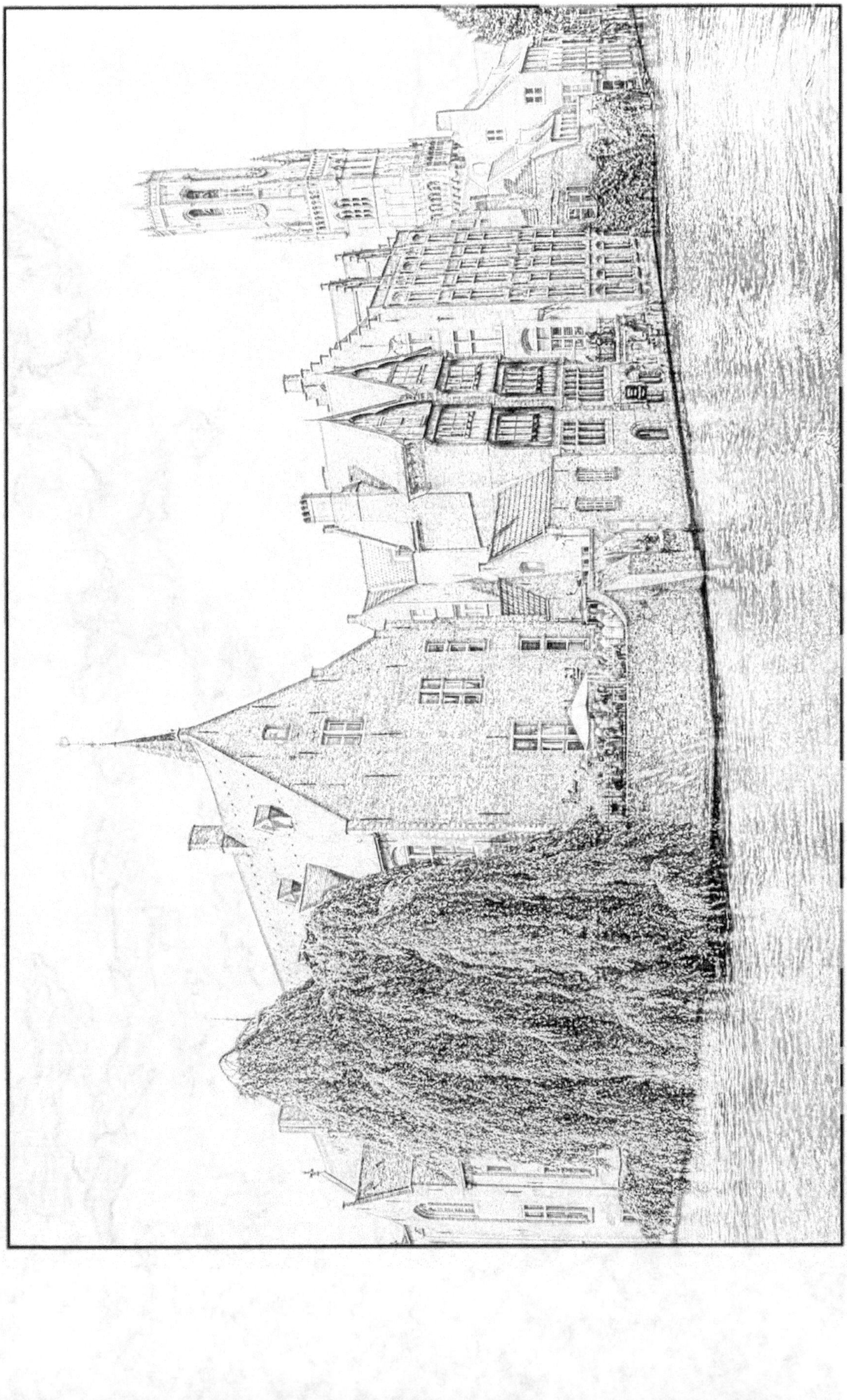

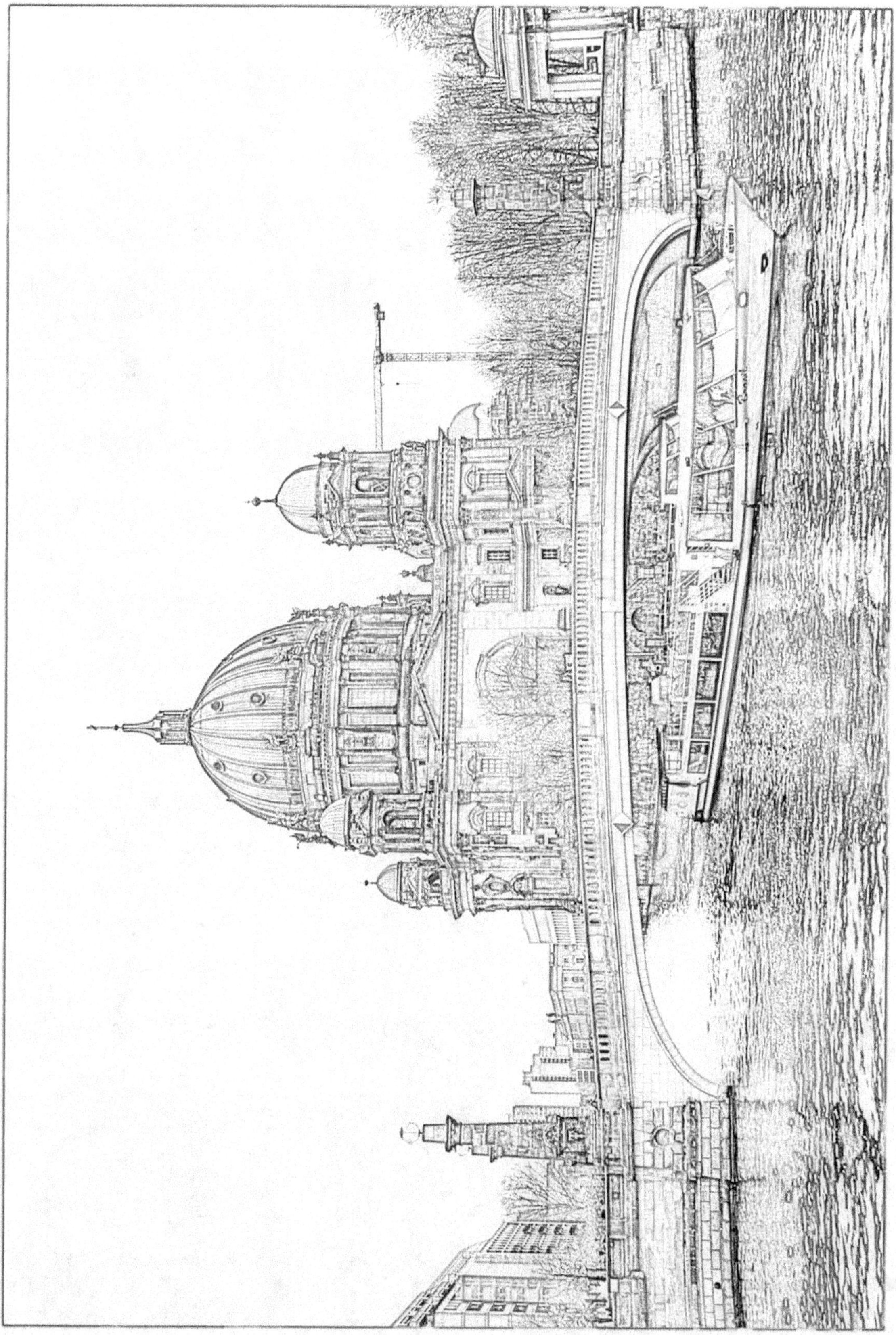

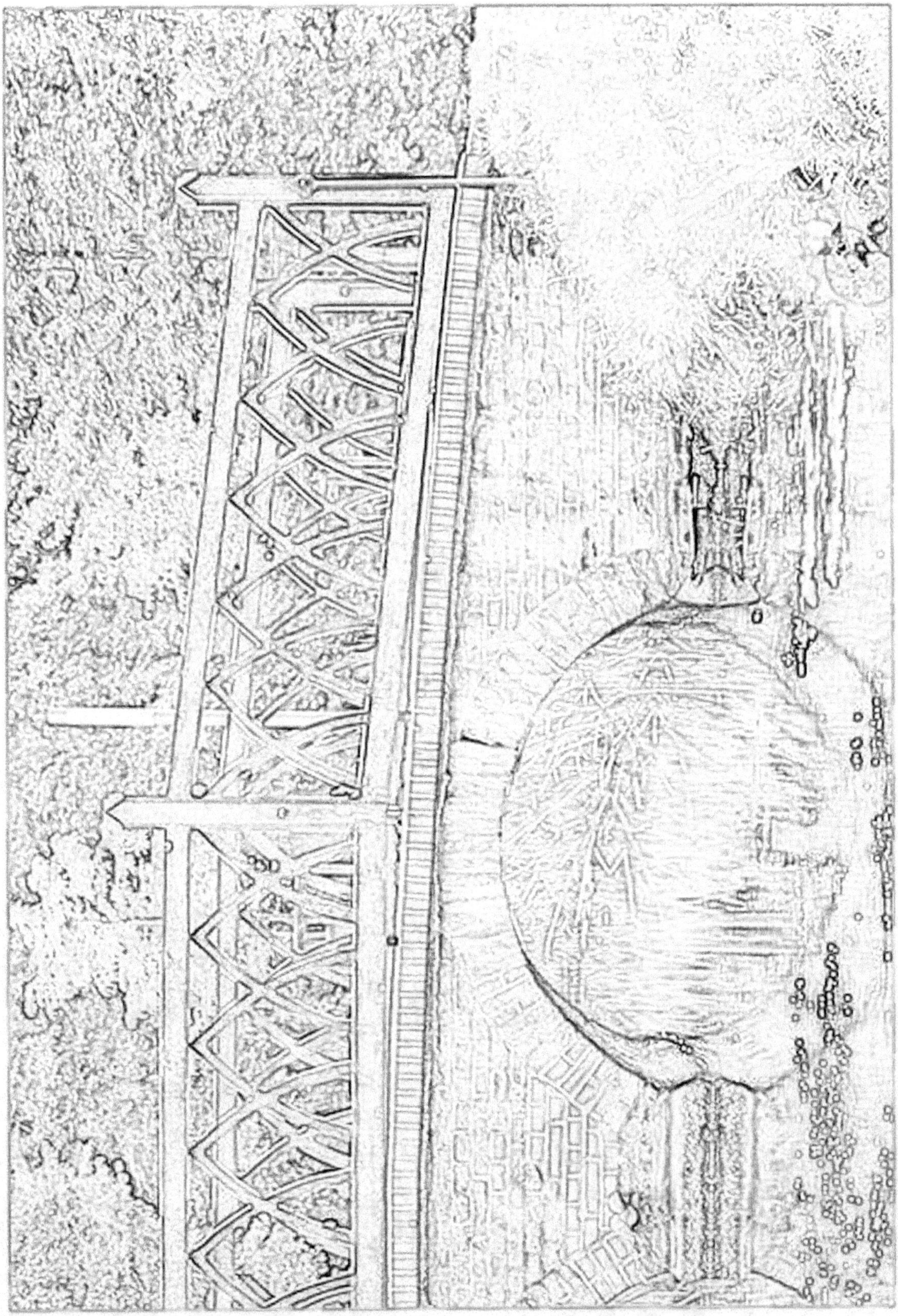

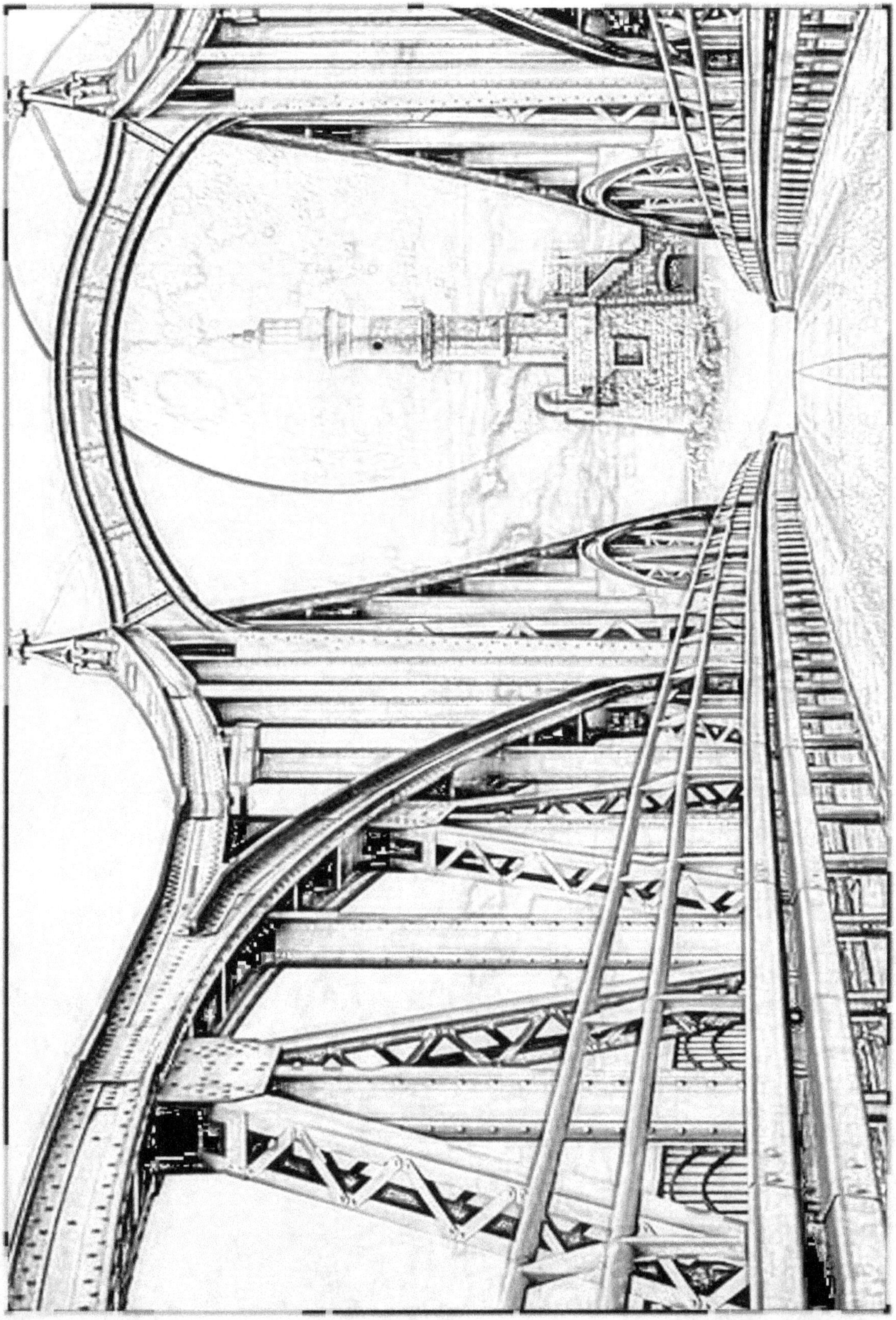

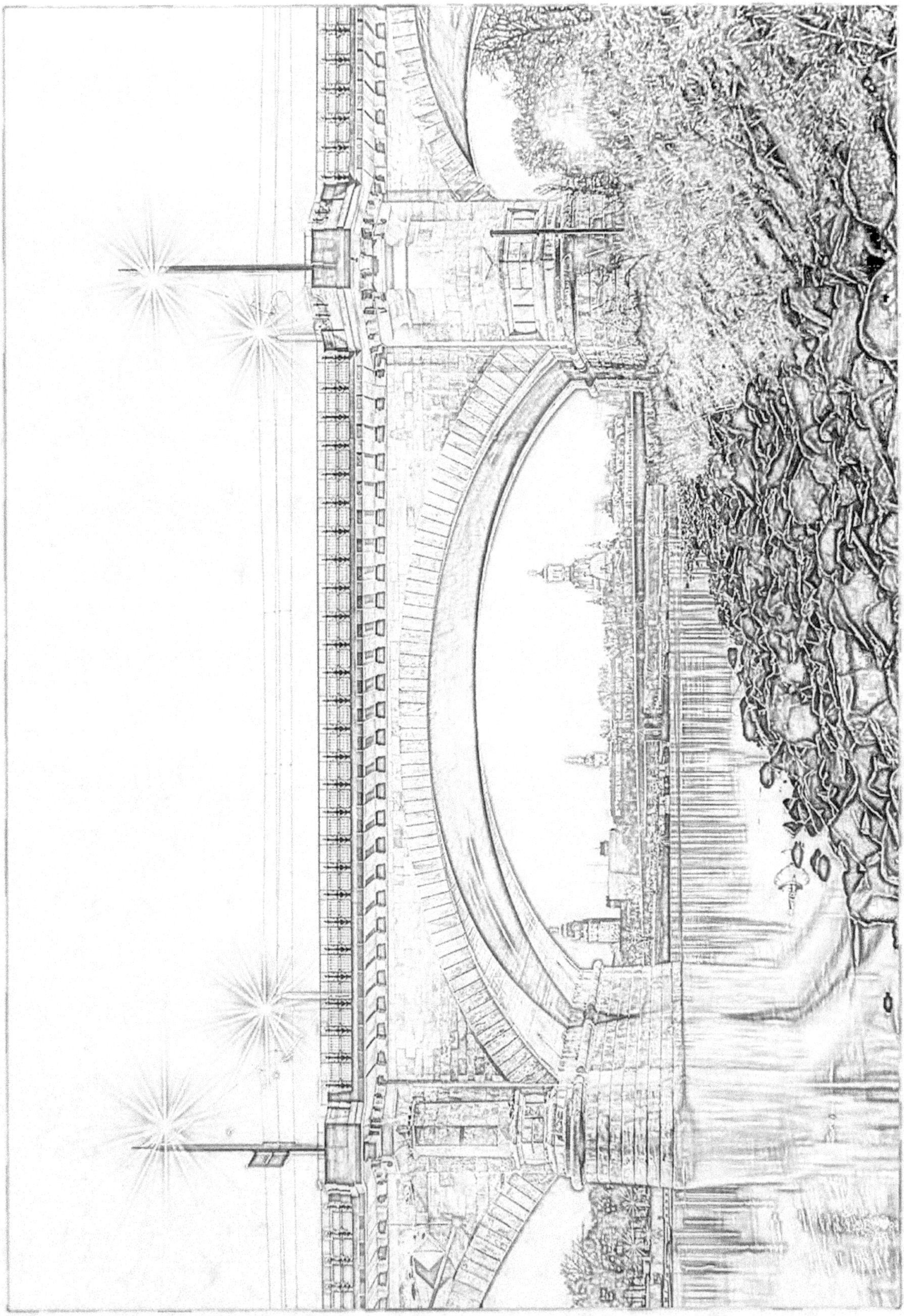

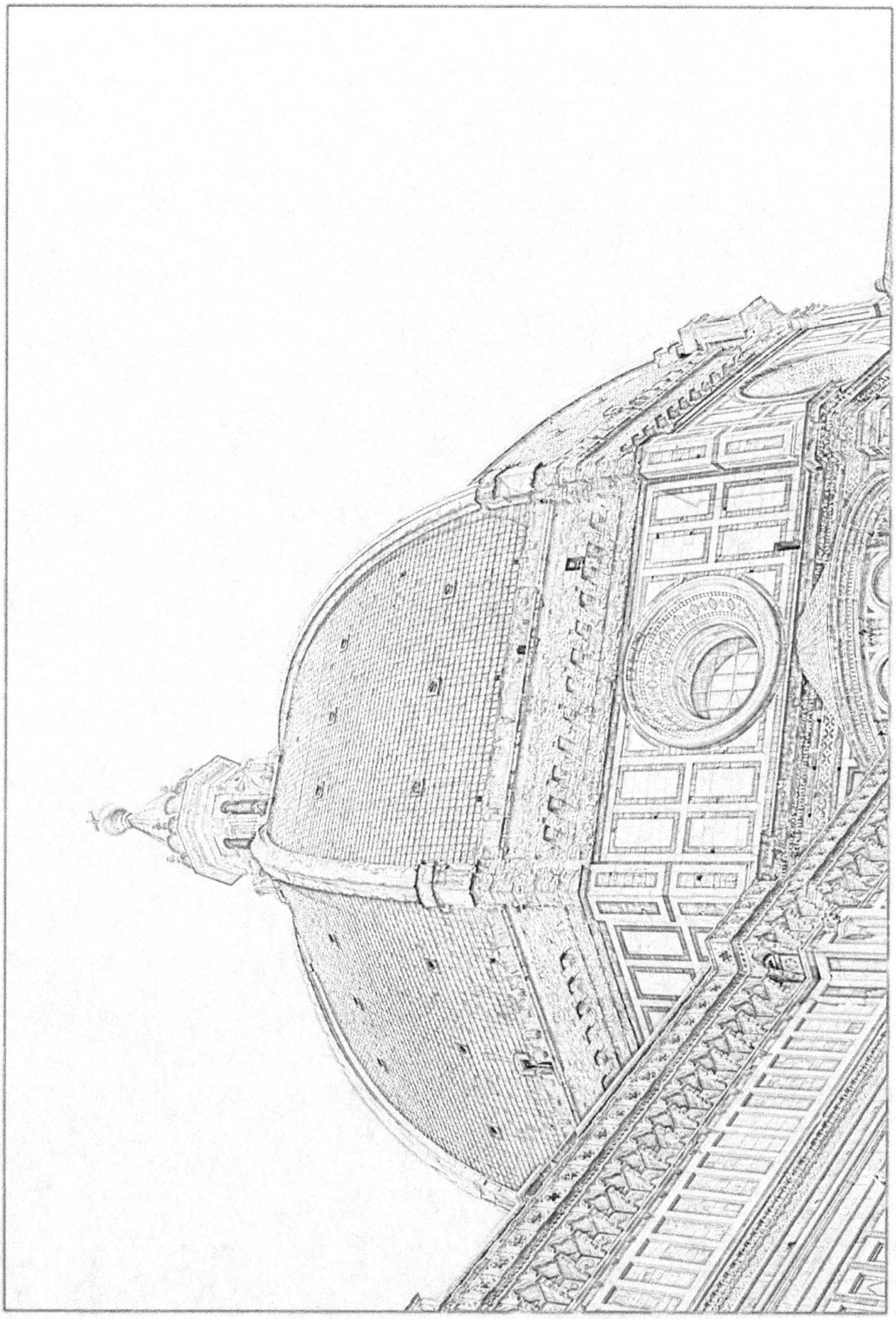

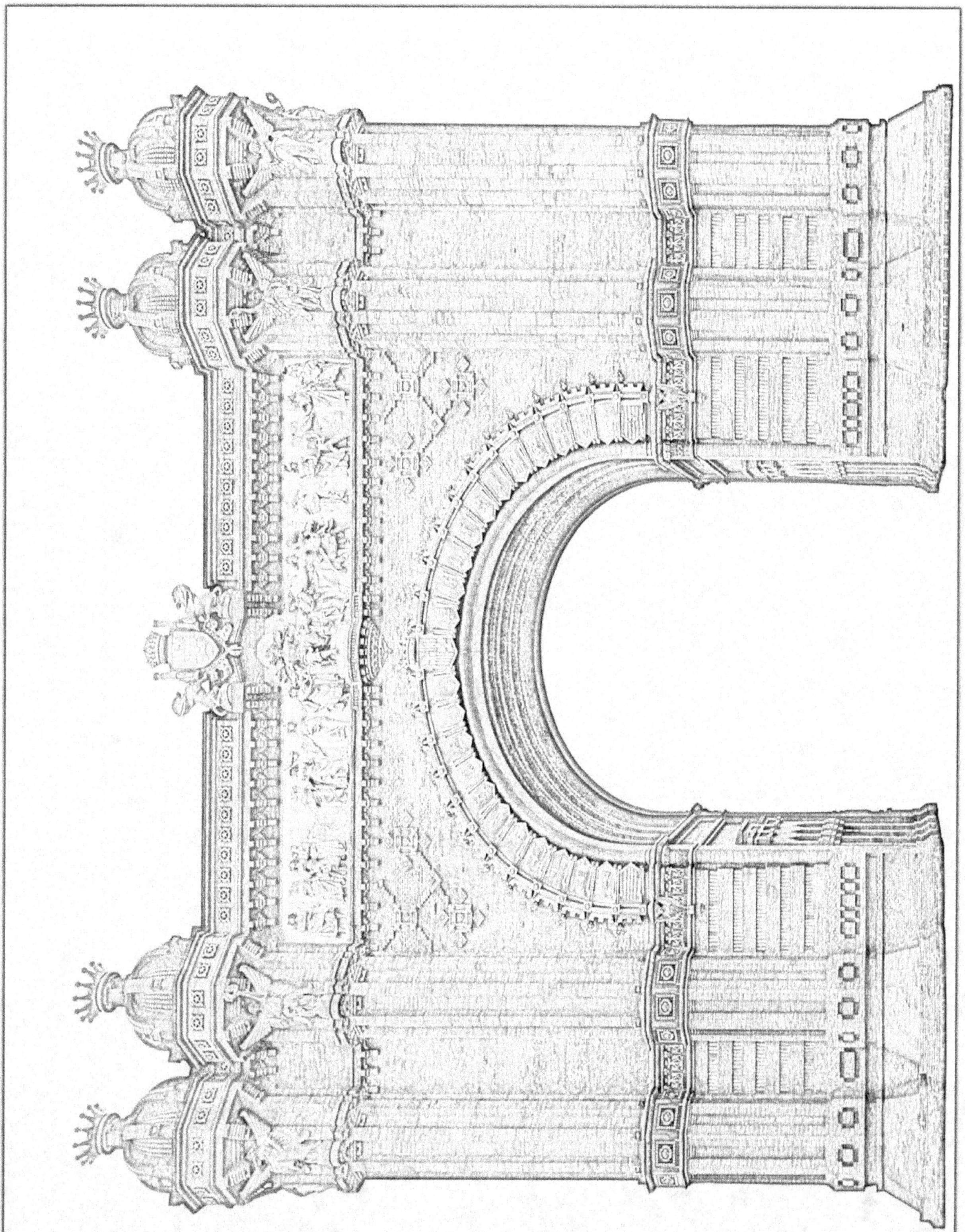

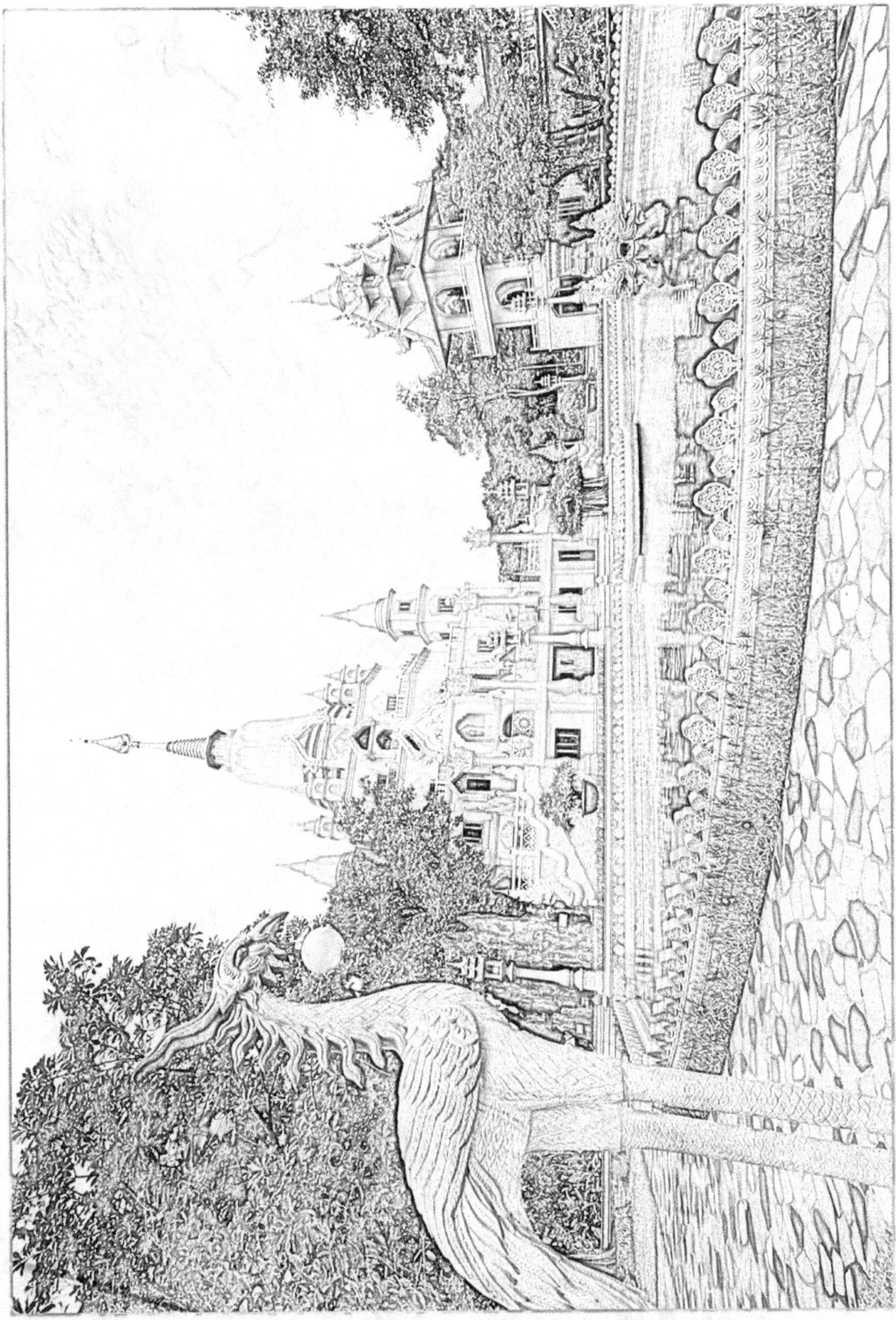

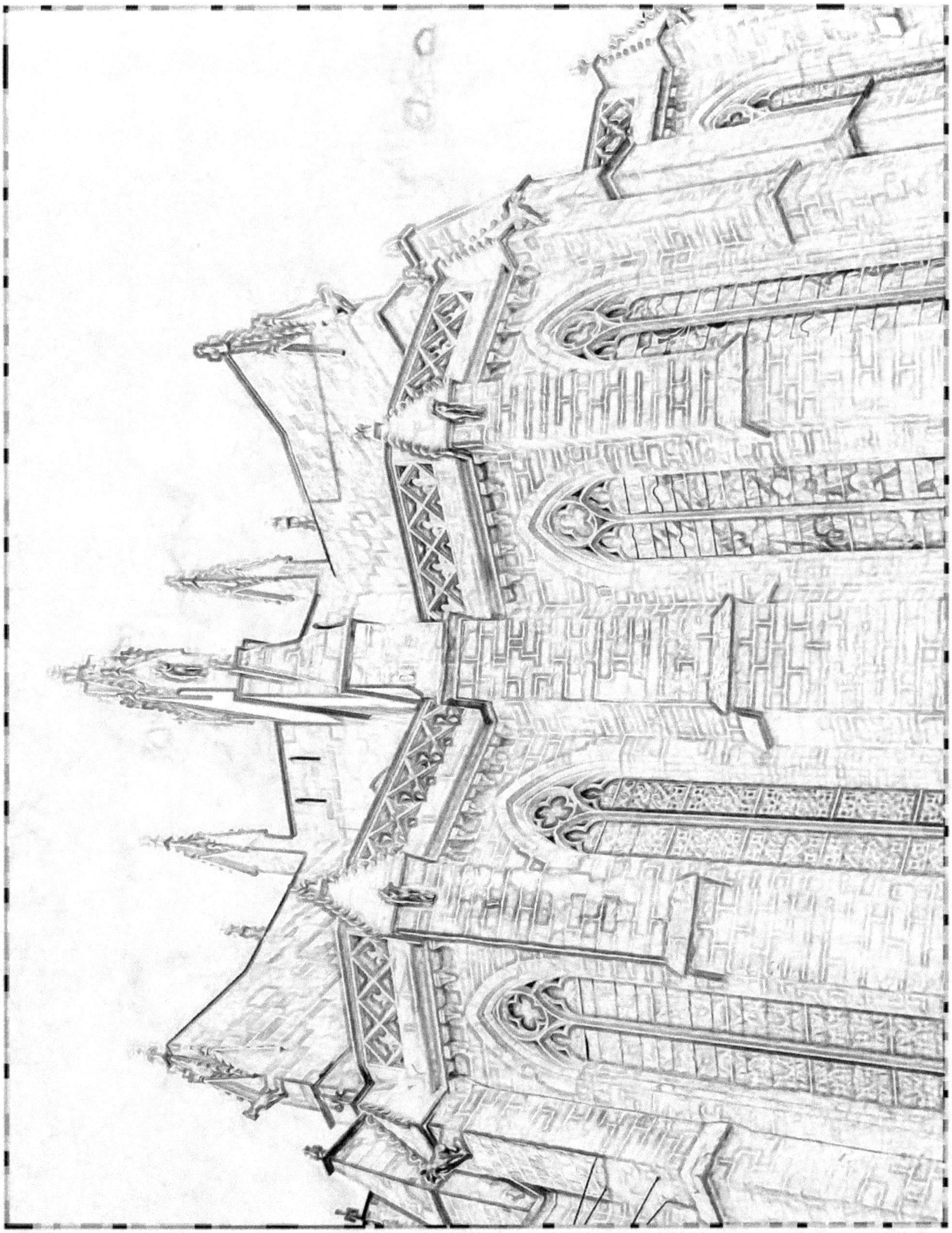

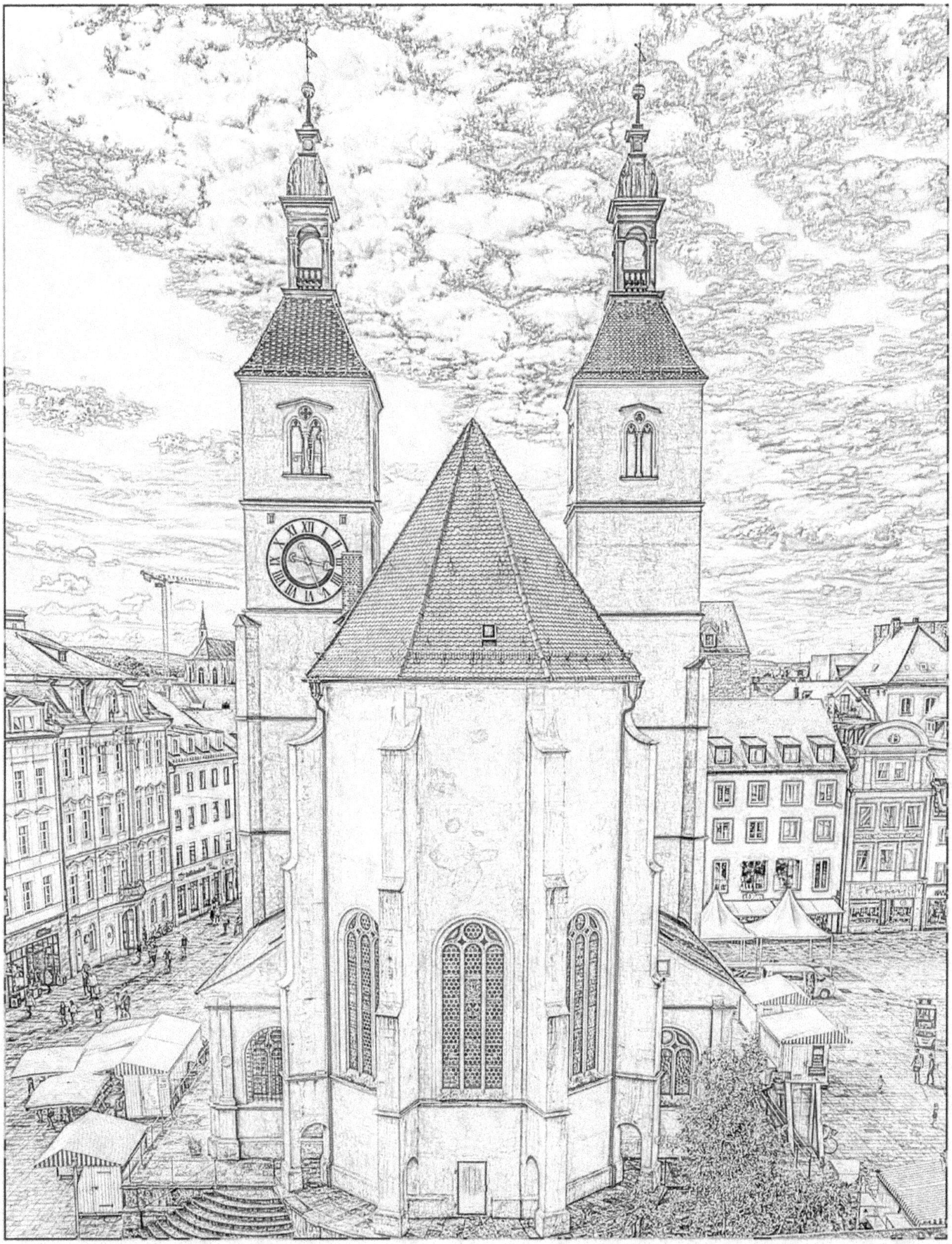

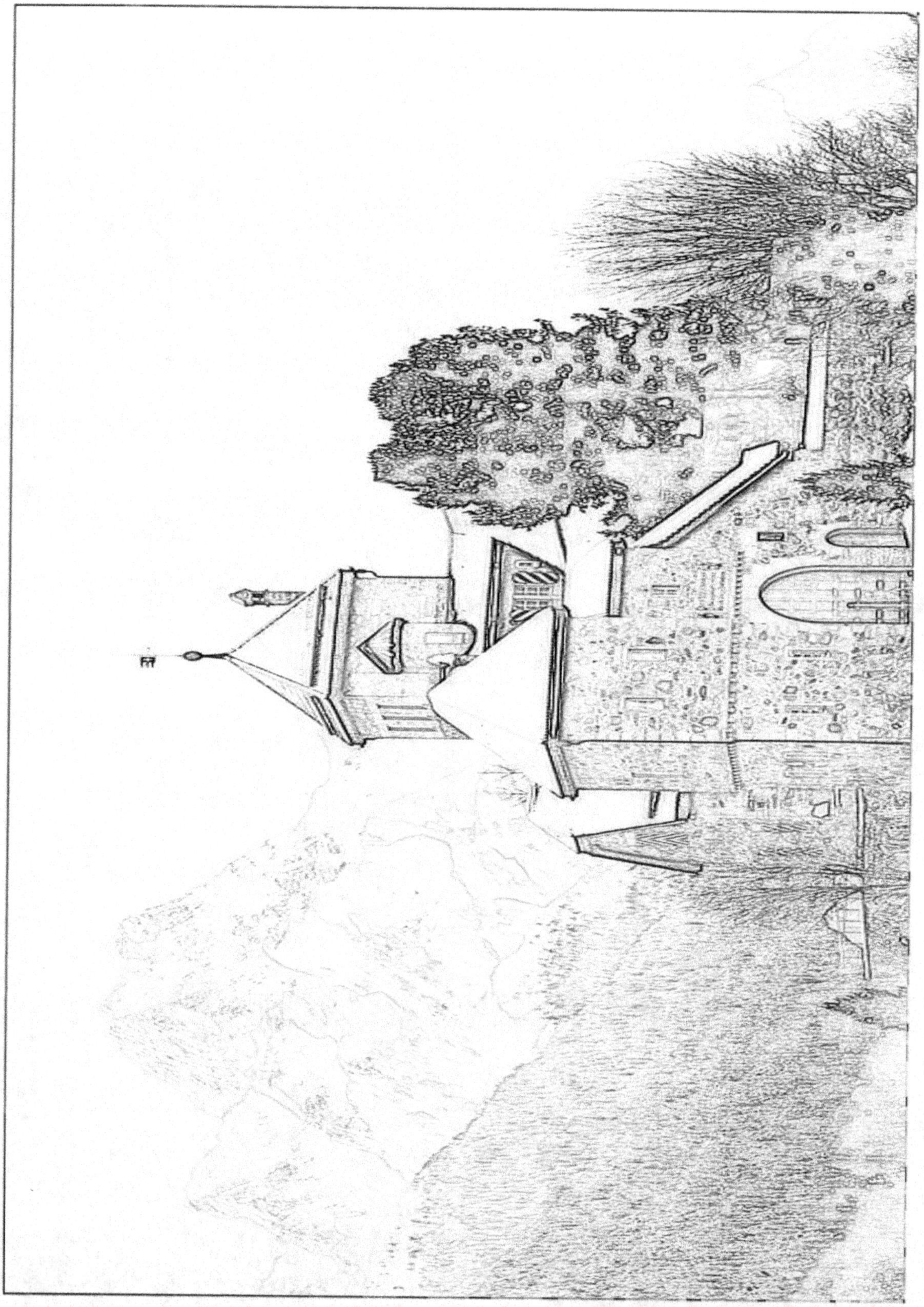

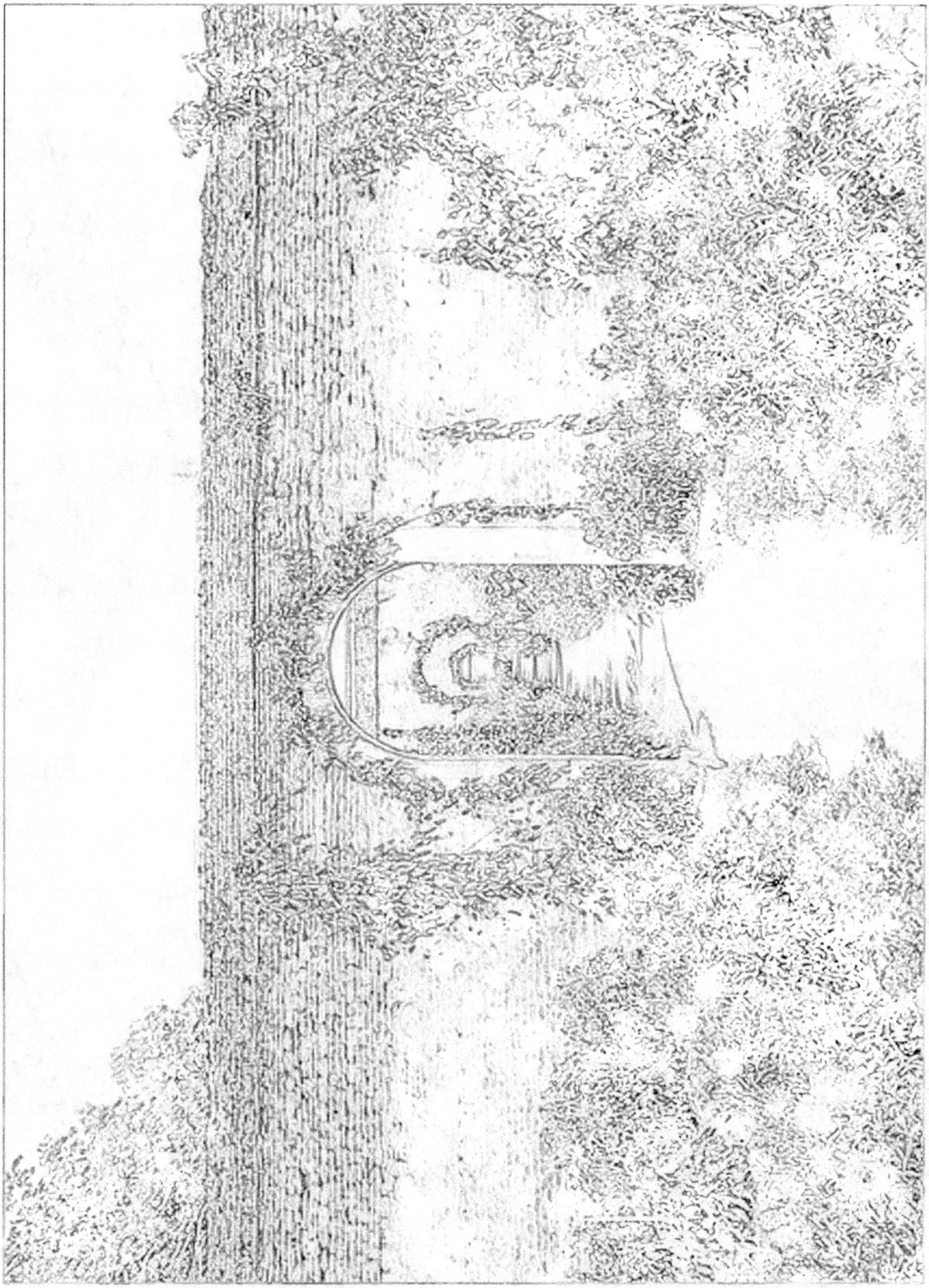

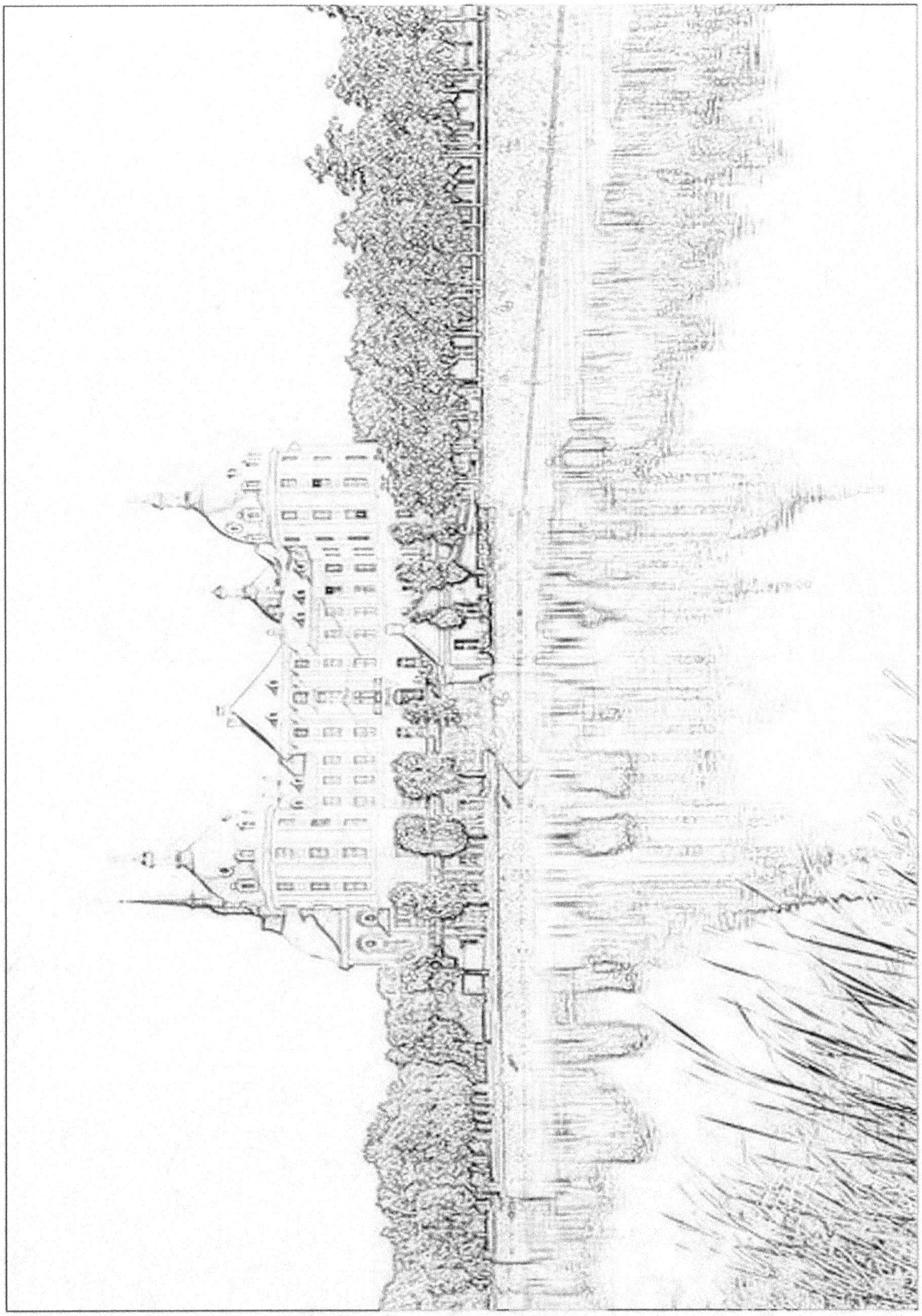

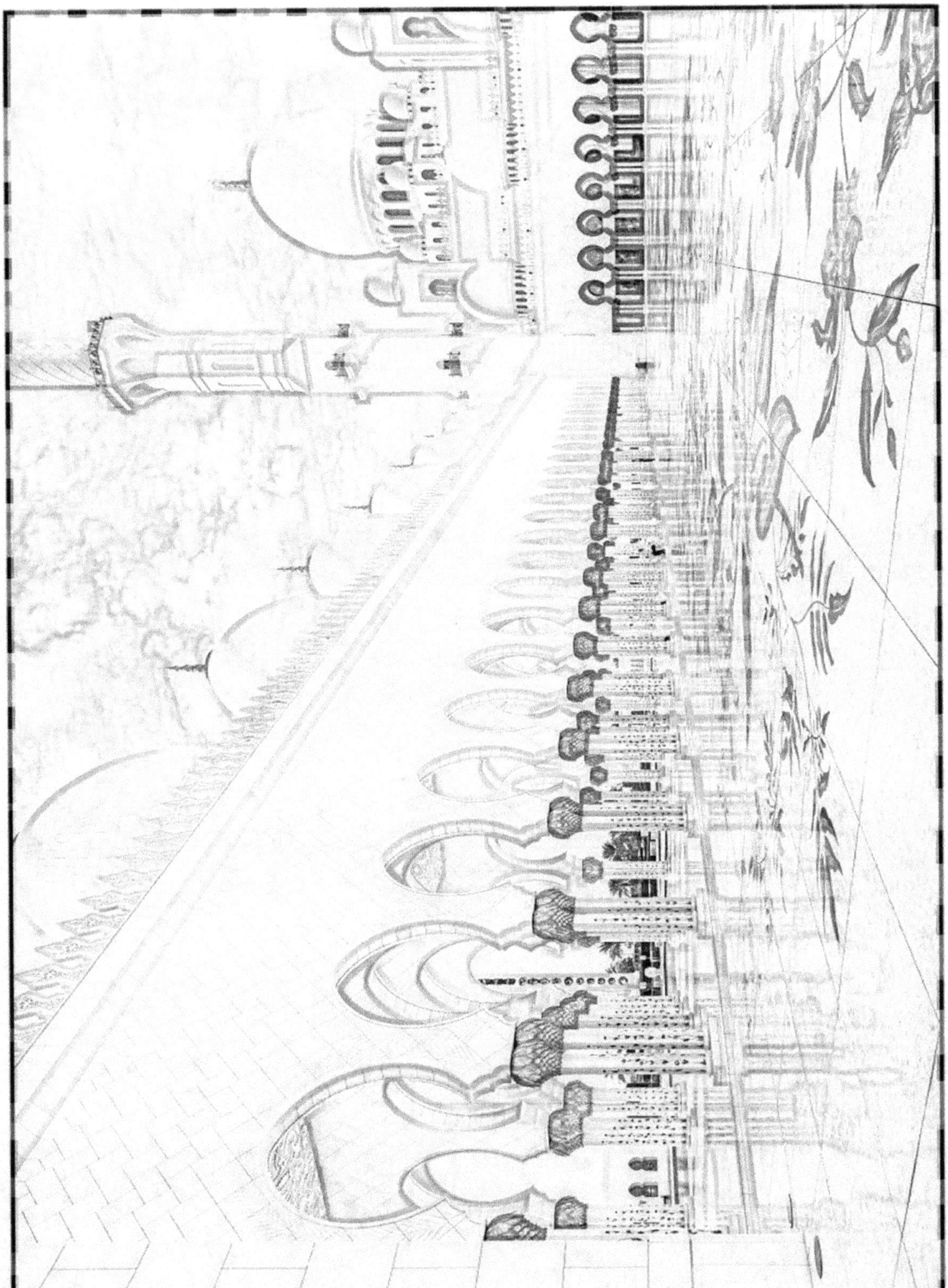

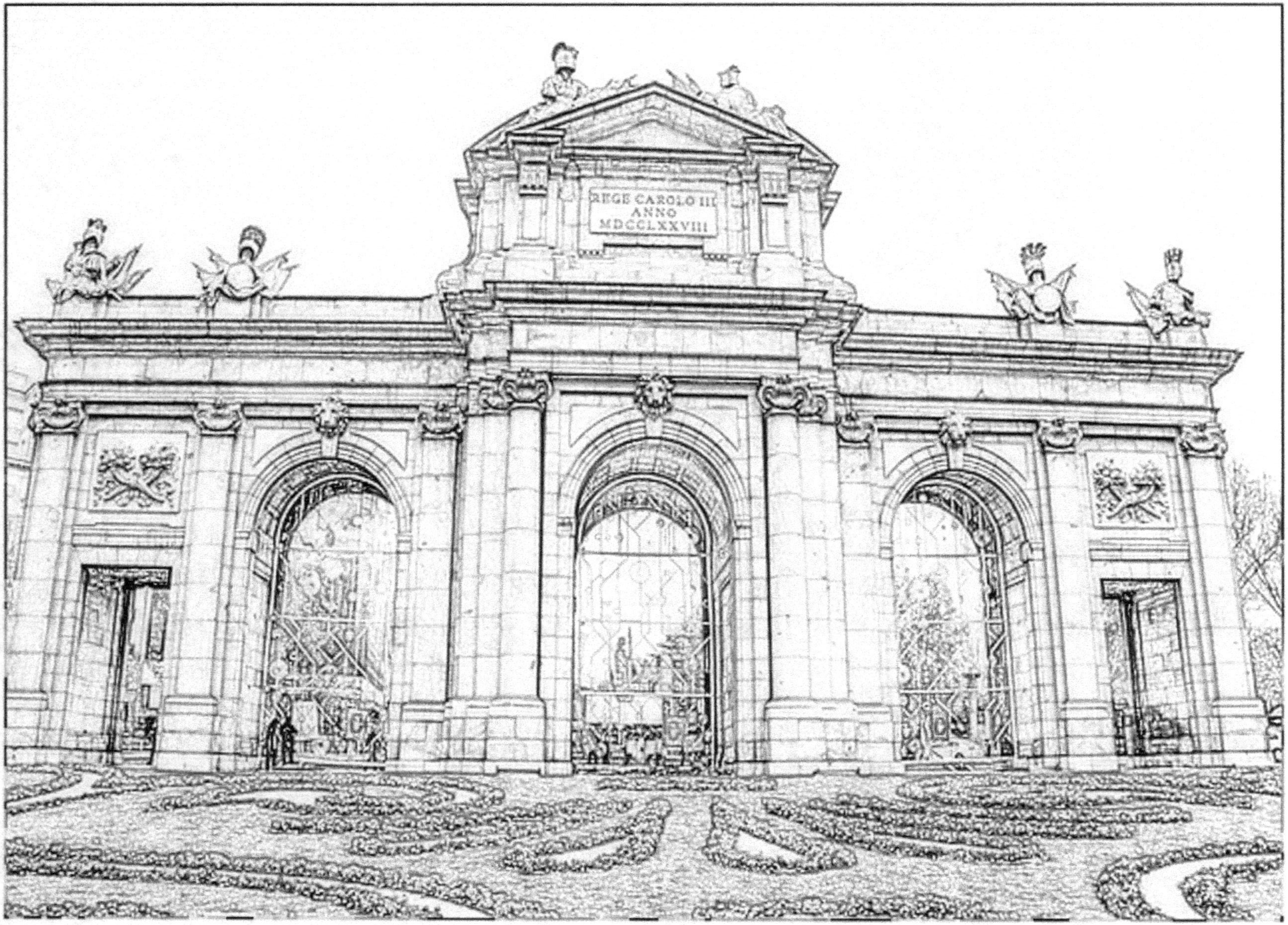
REGE CAROLO III
ANNO
MDCCLXXVIII

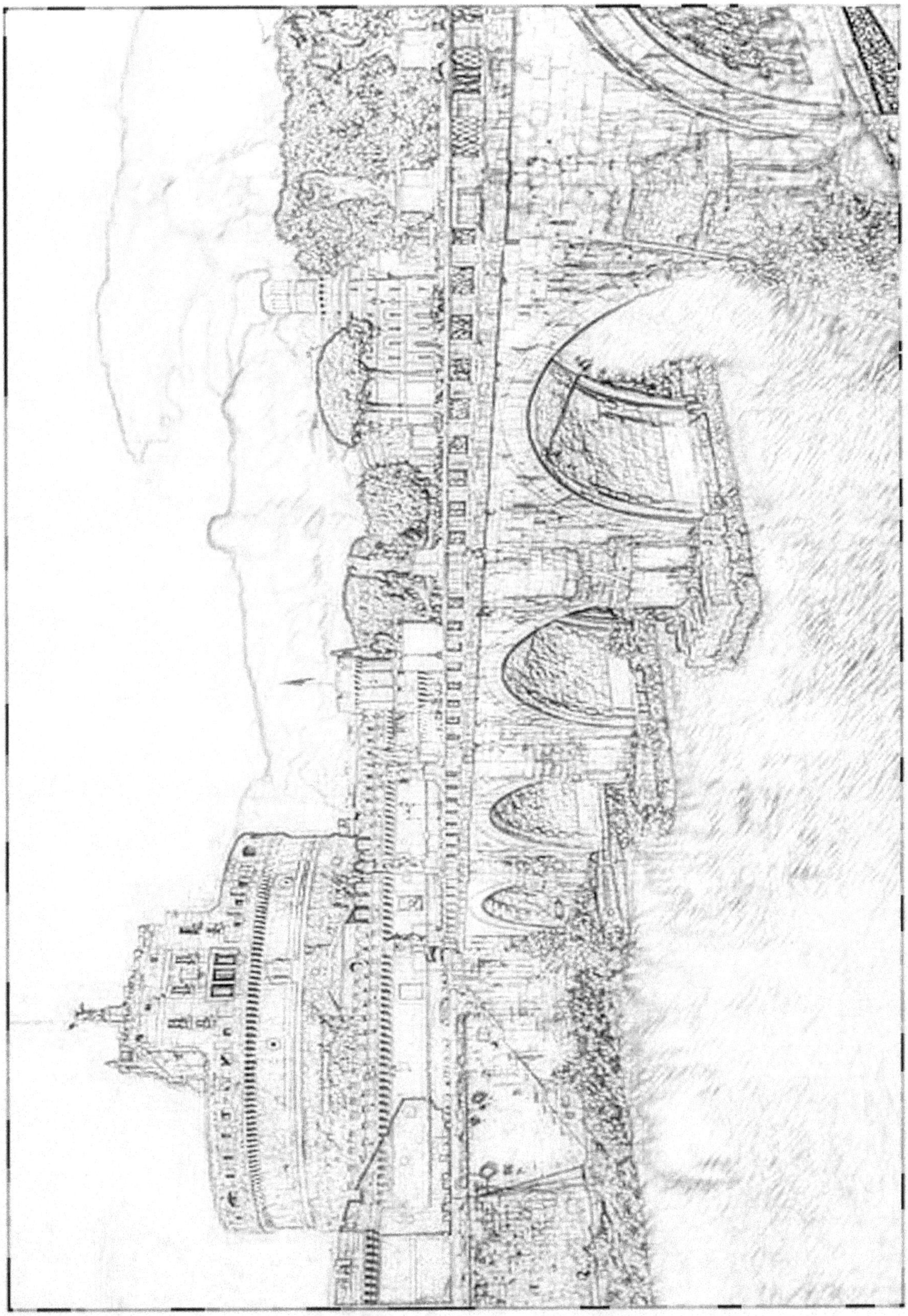

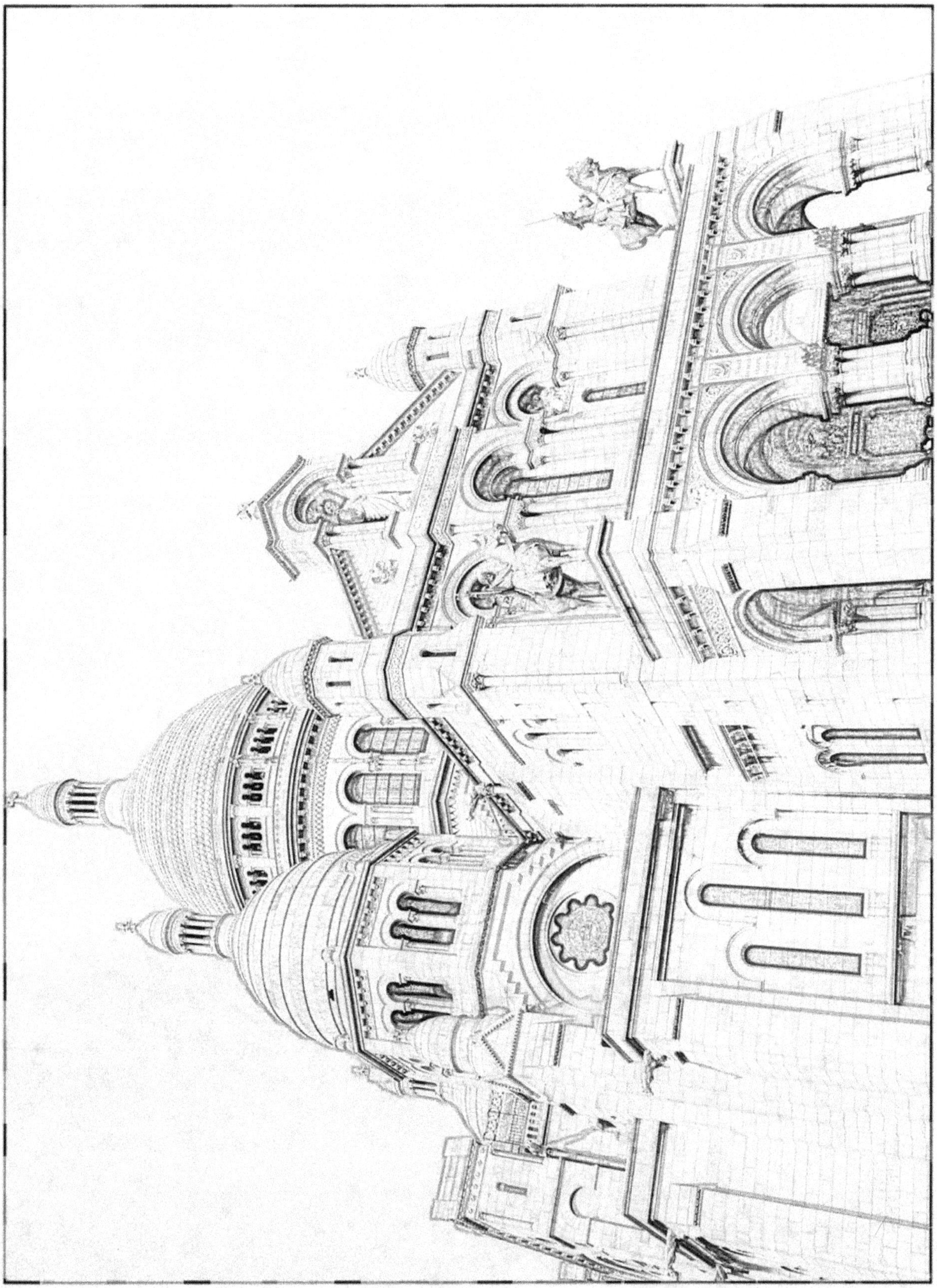

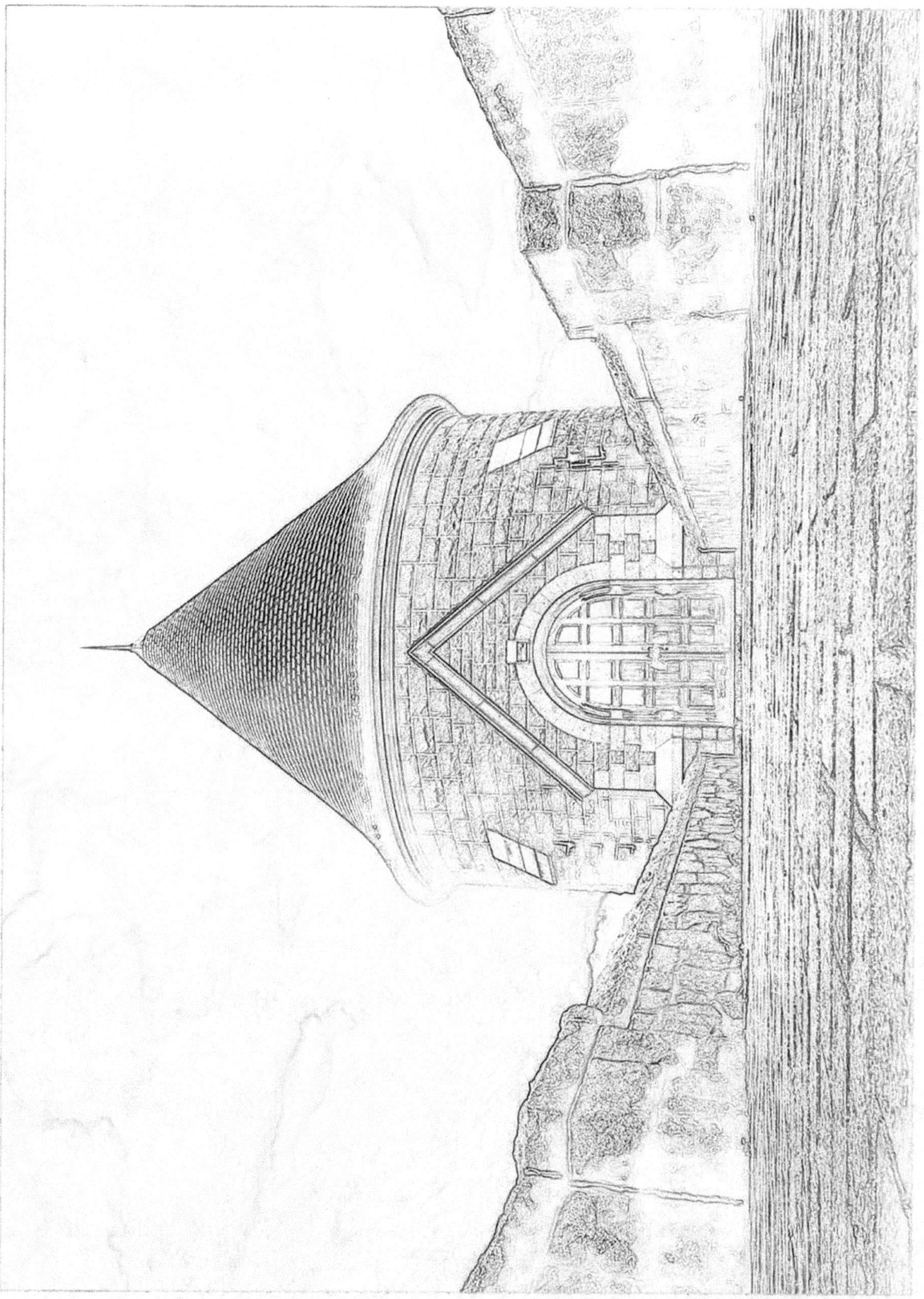

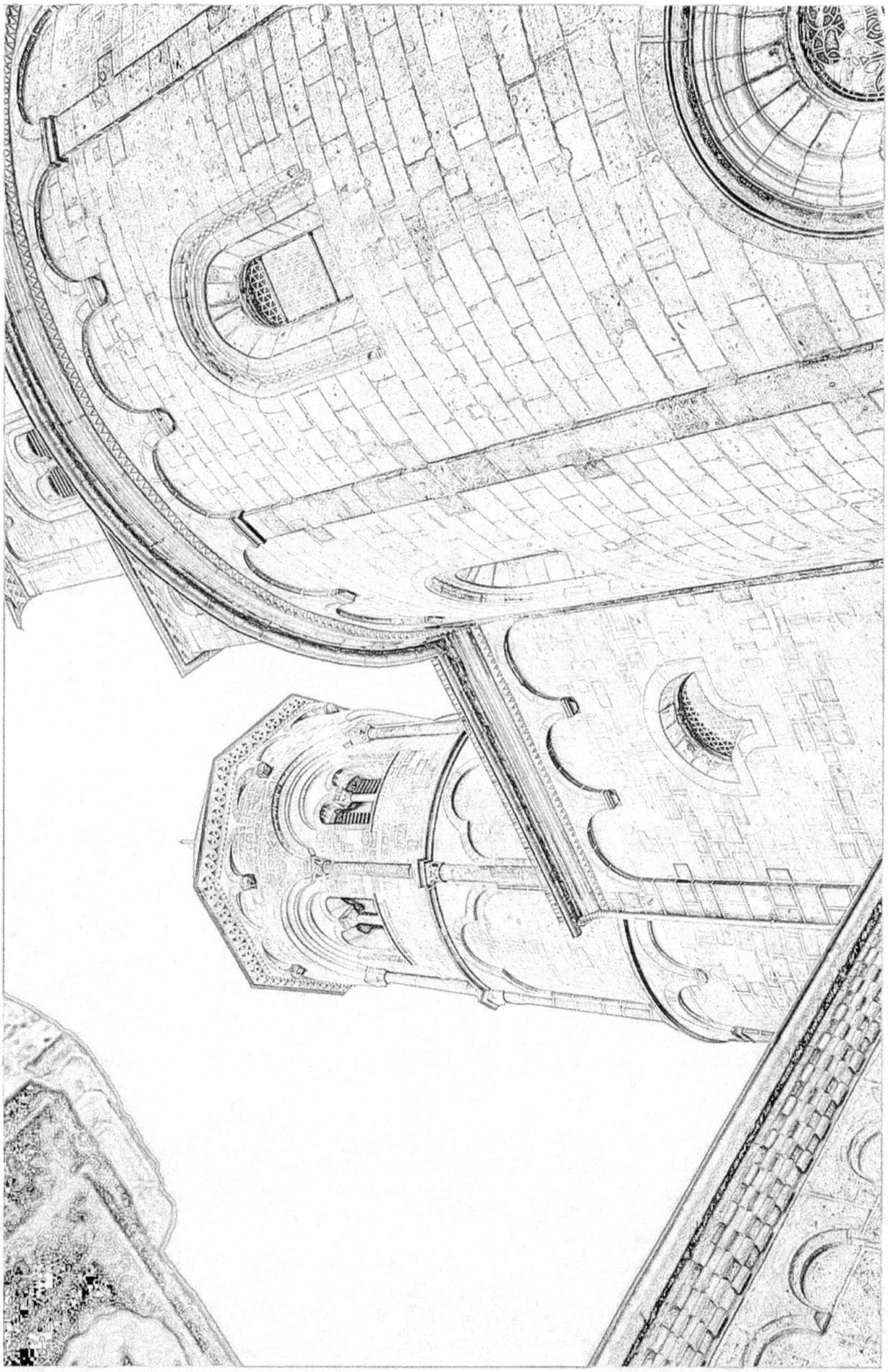

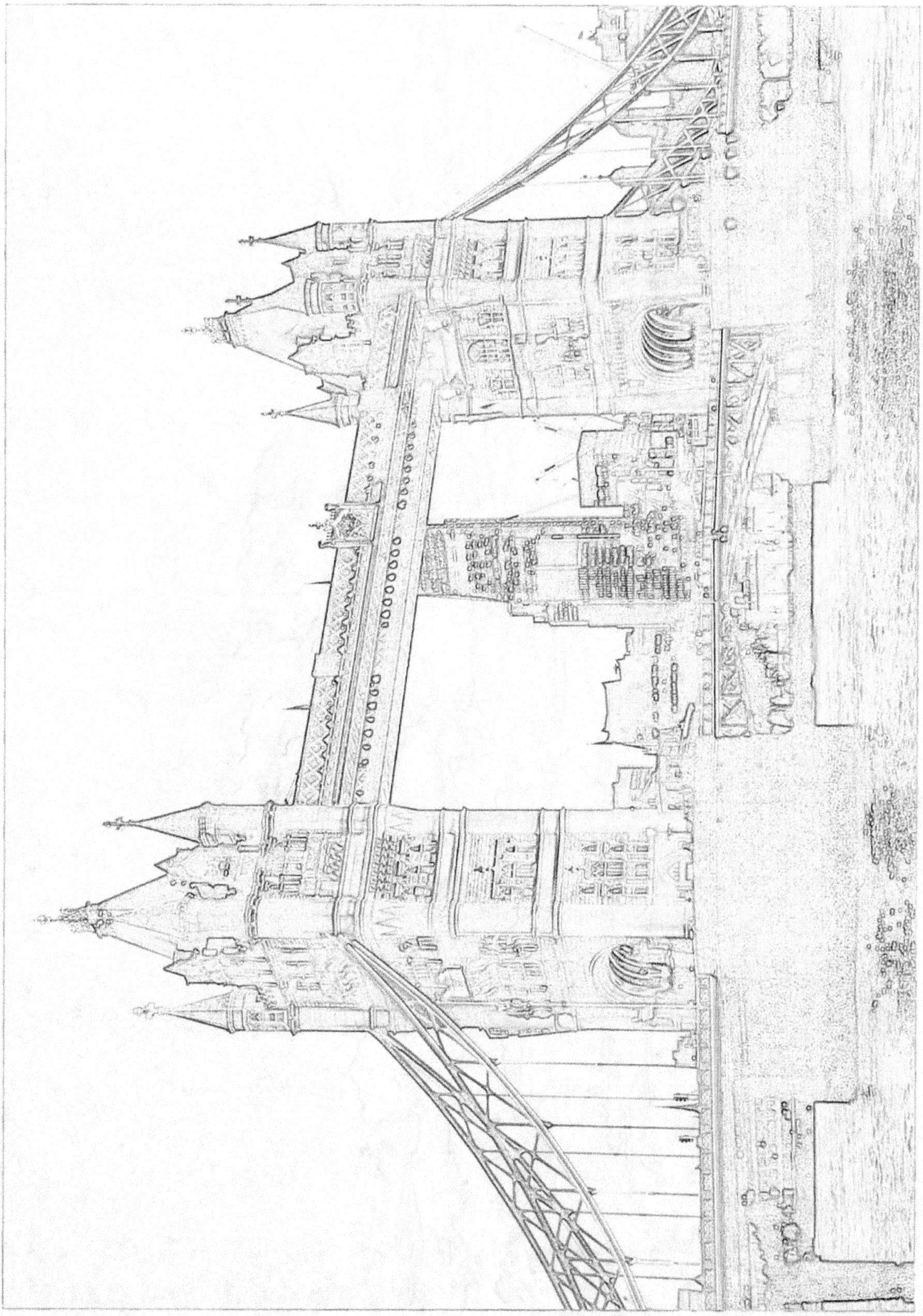

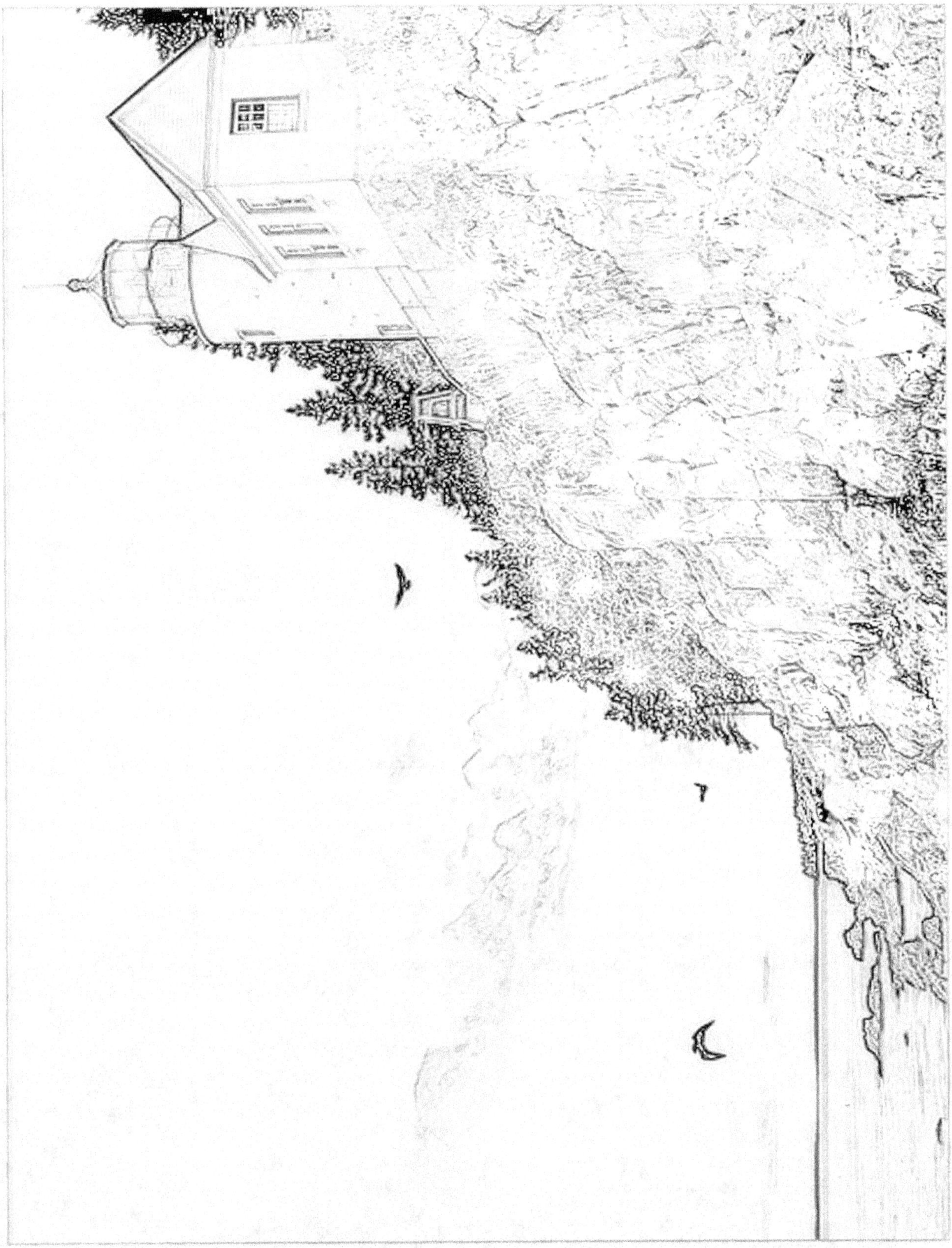

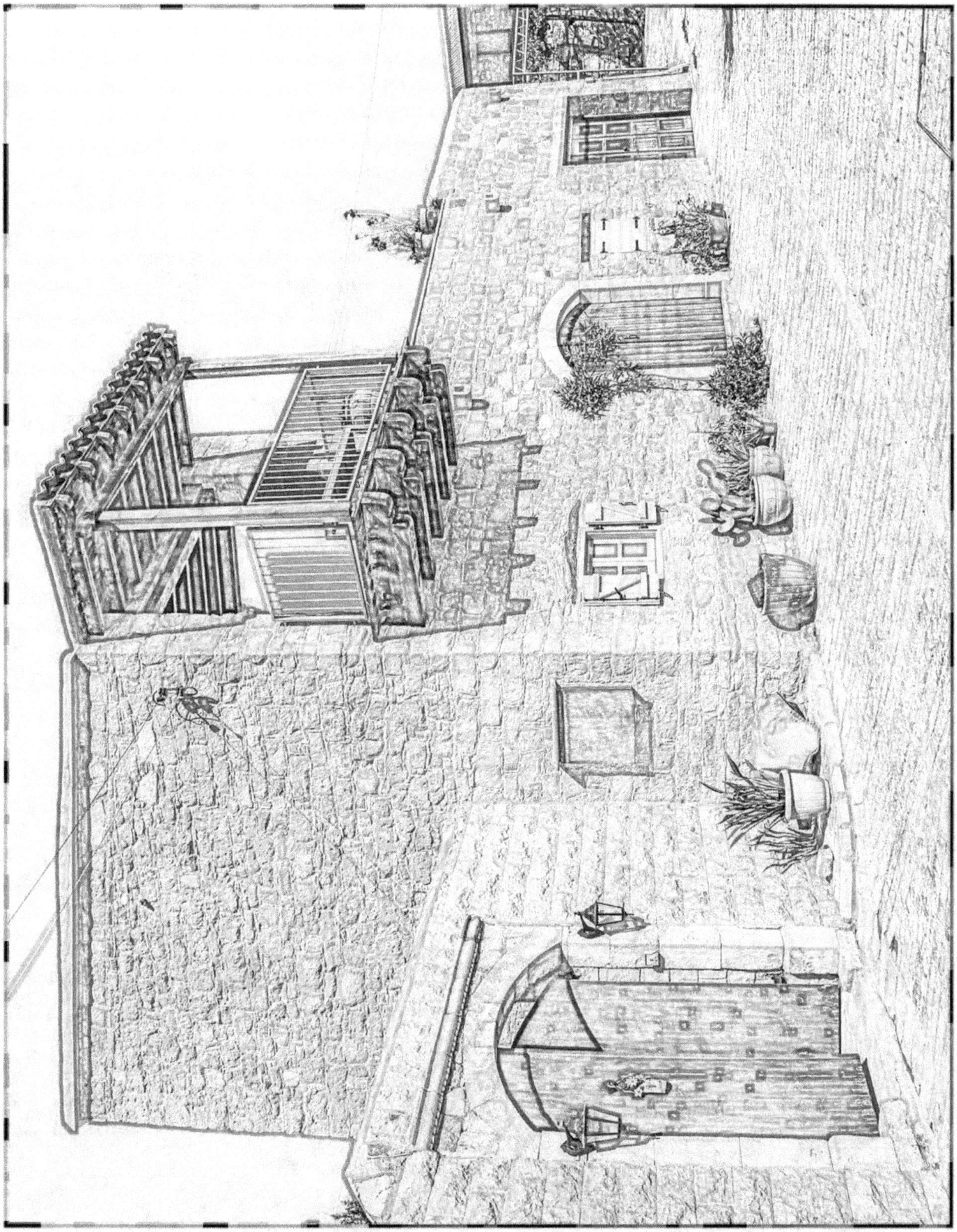

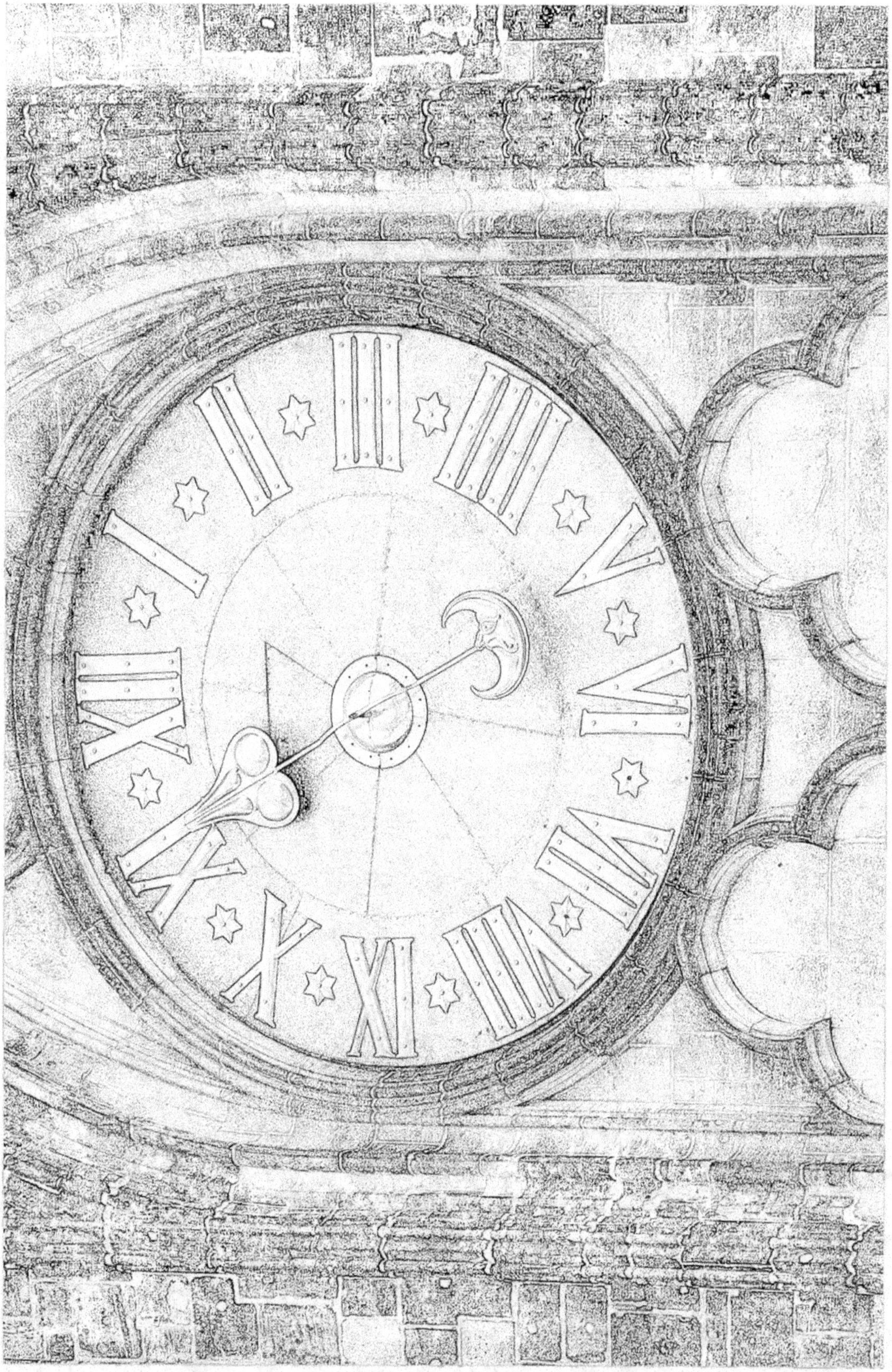

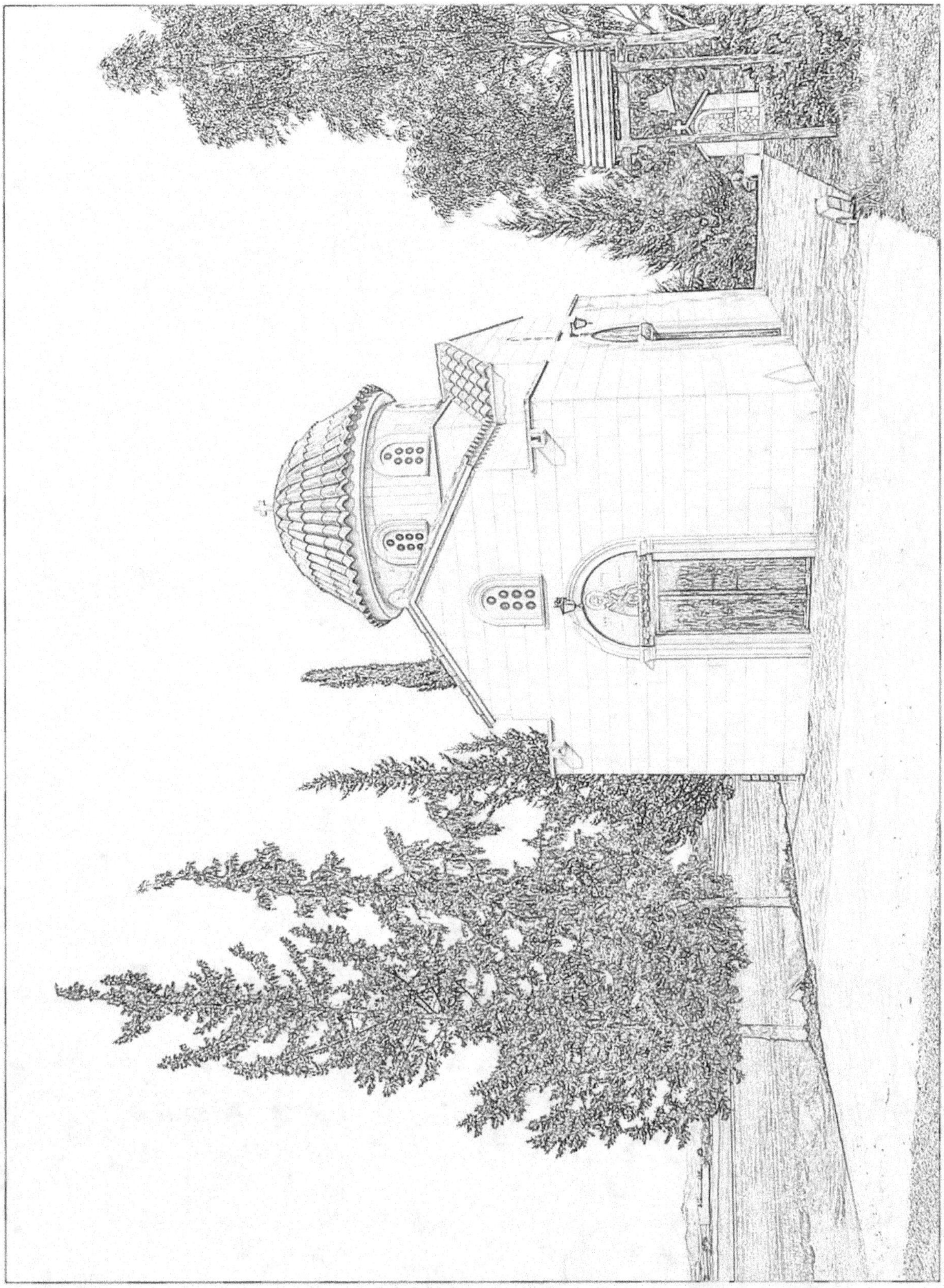

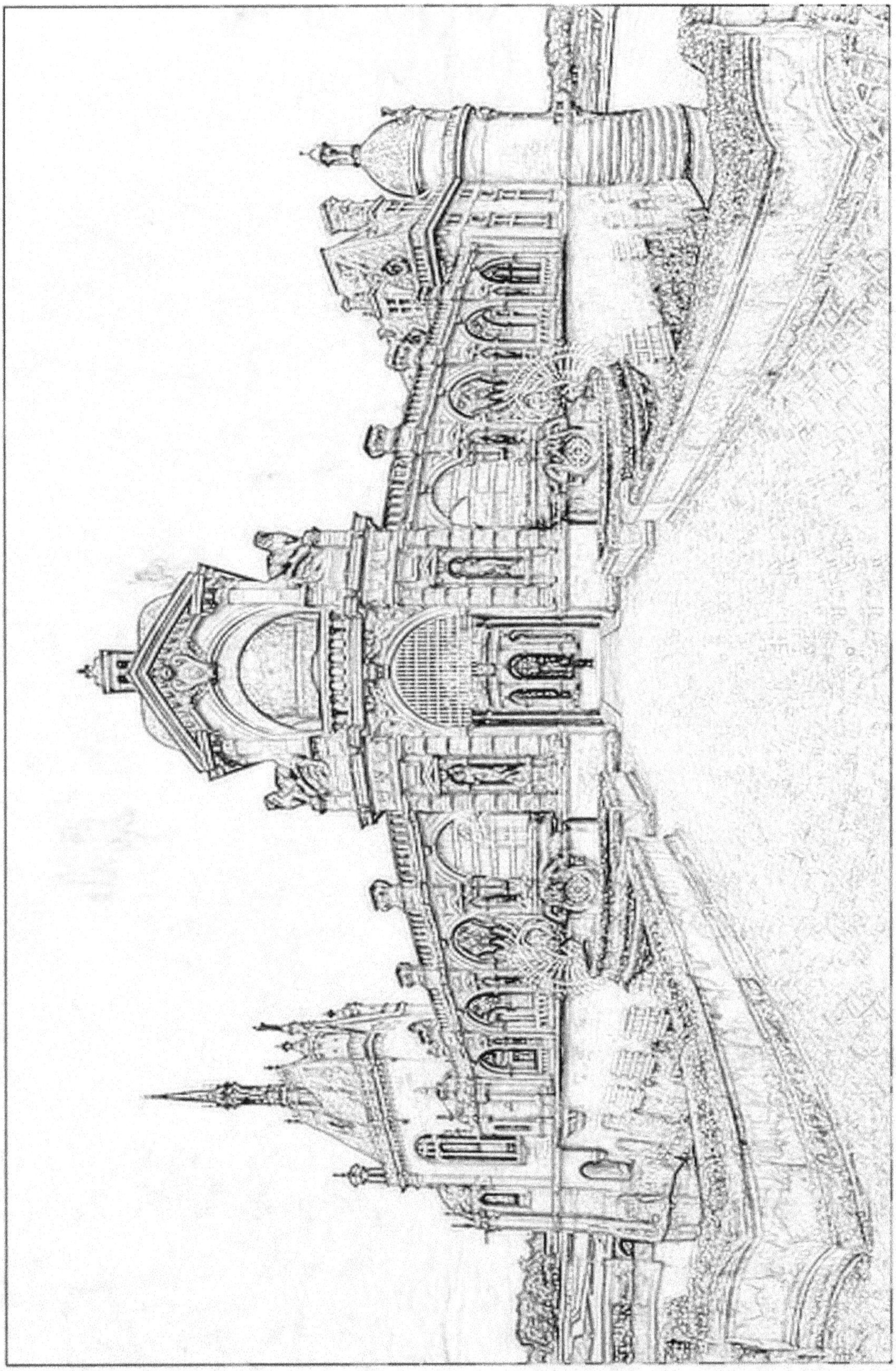

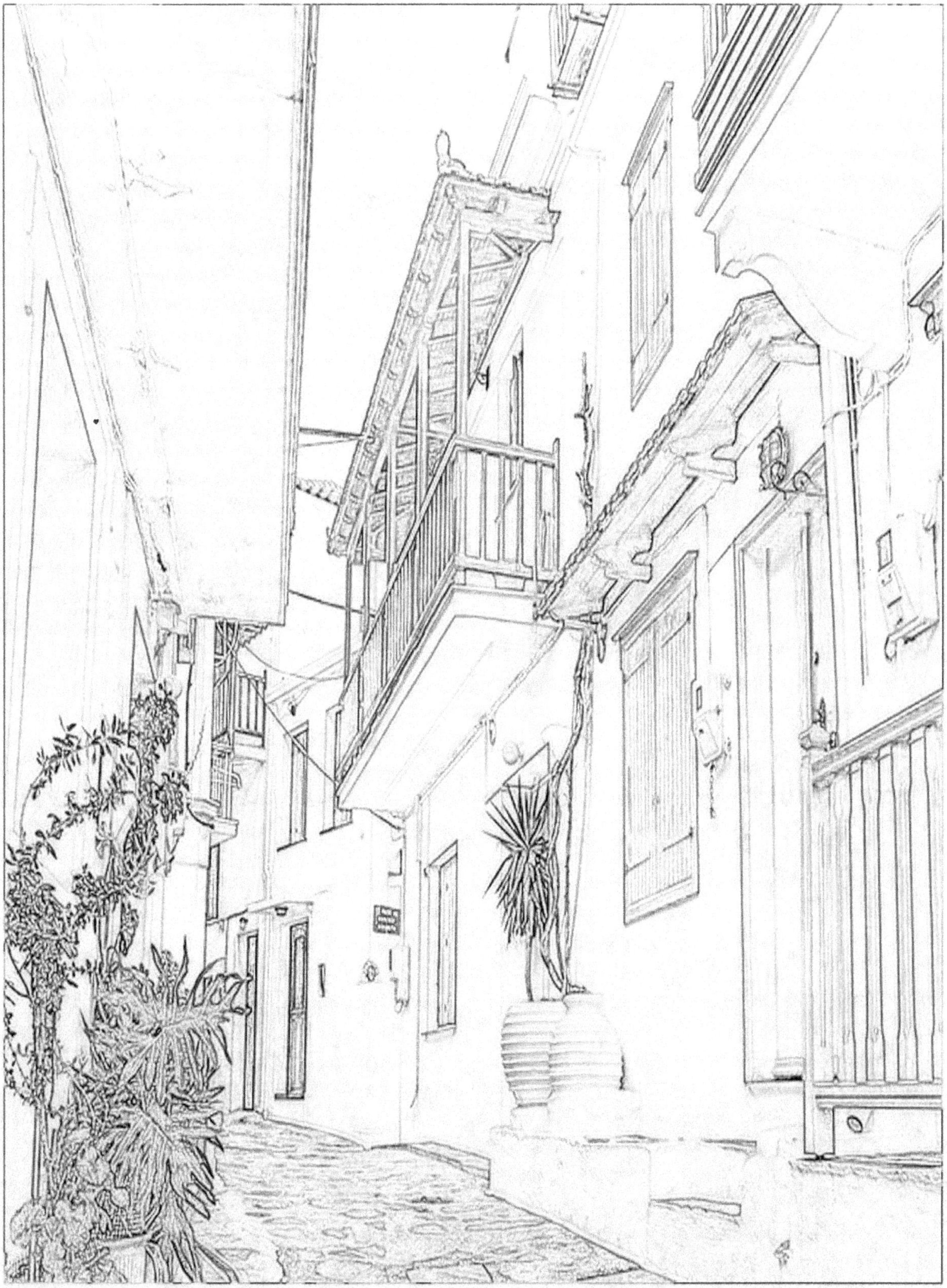

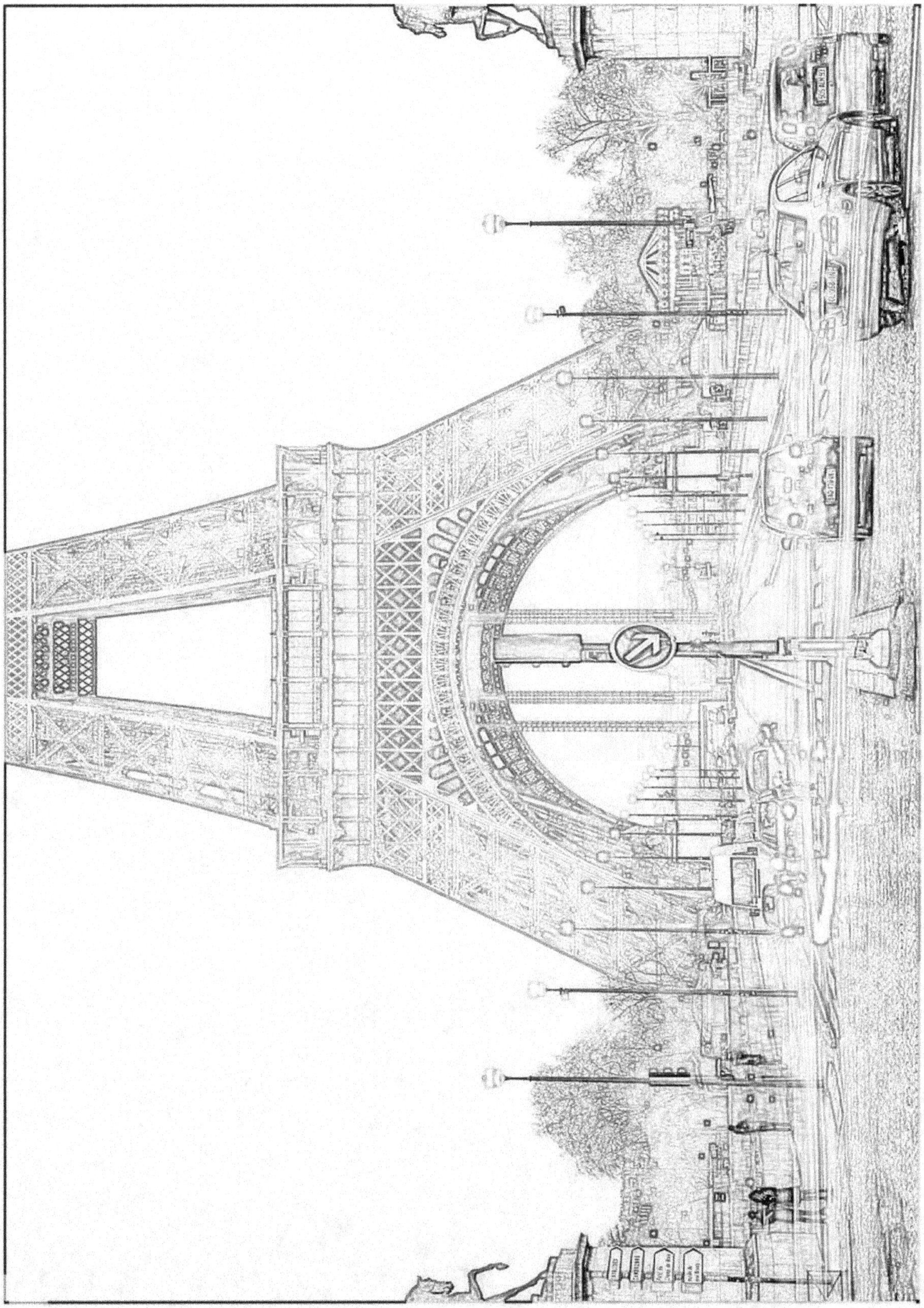

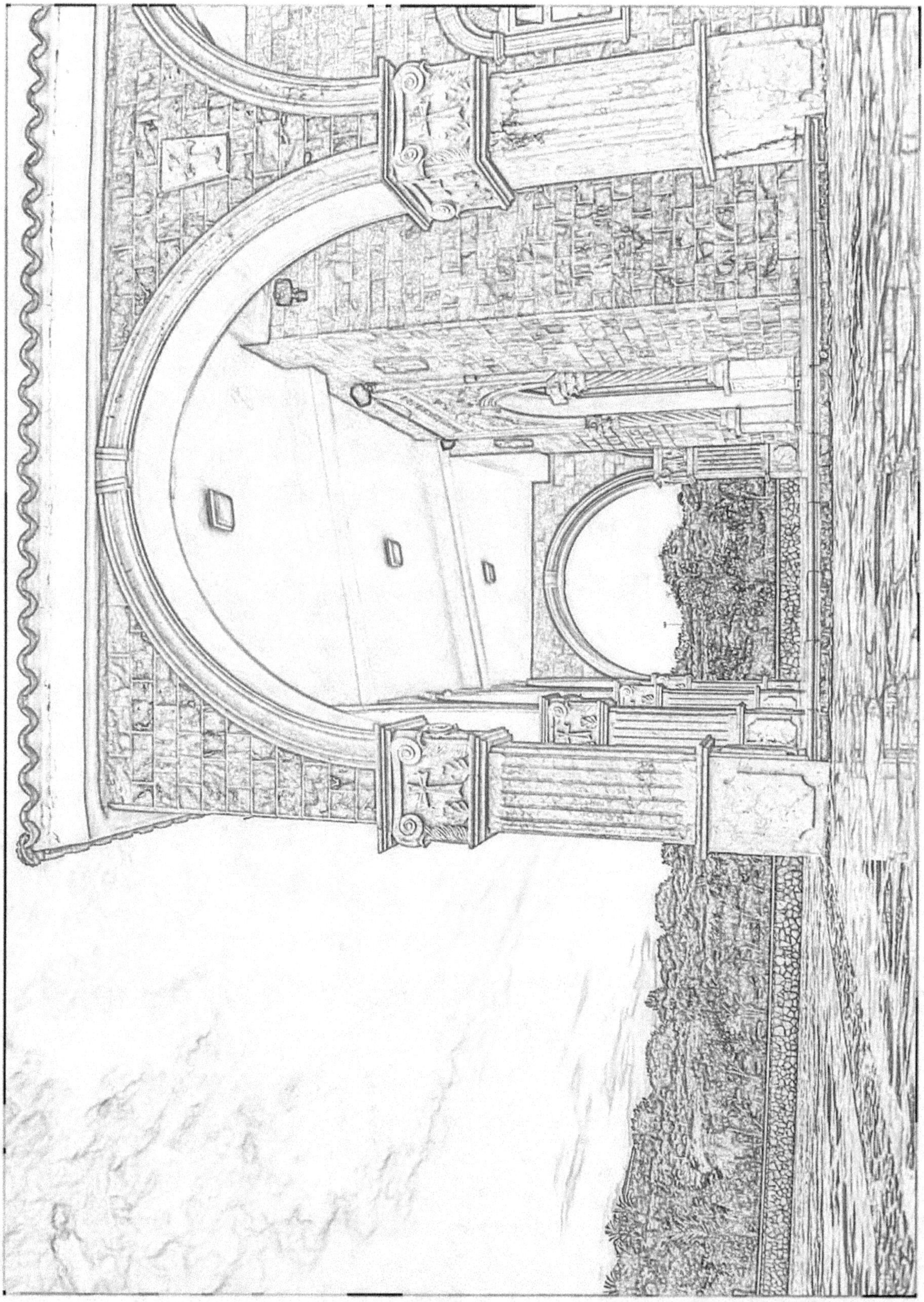

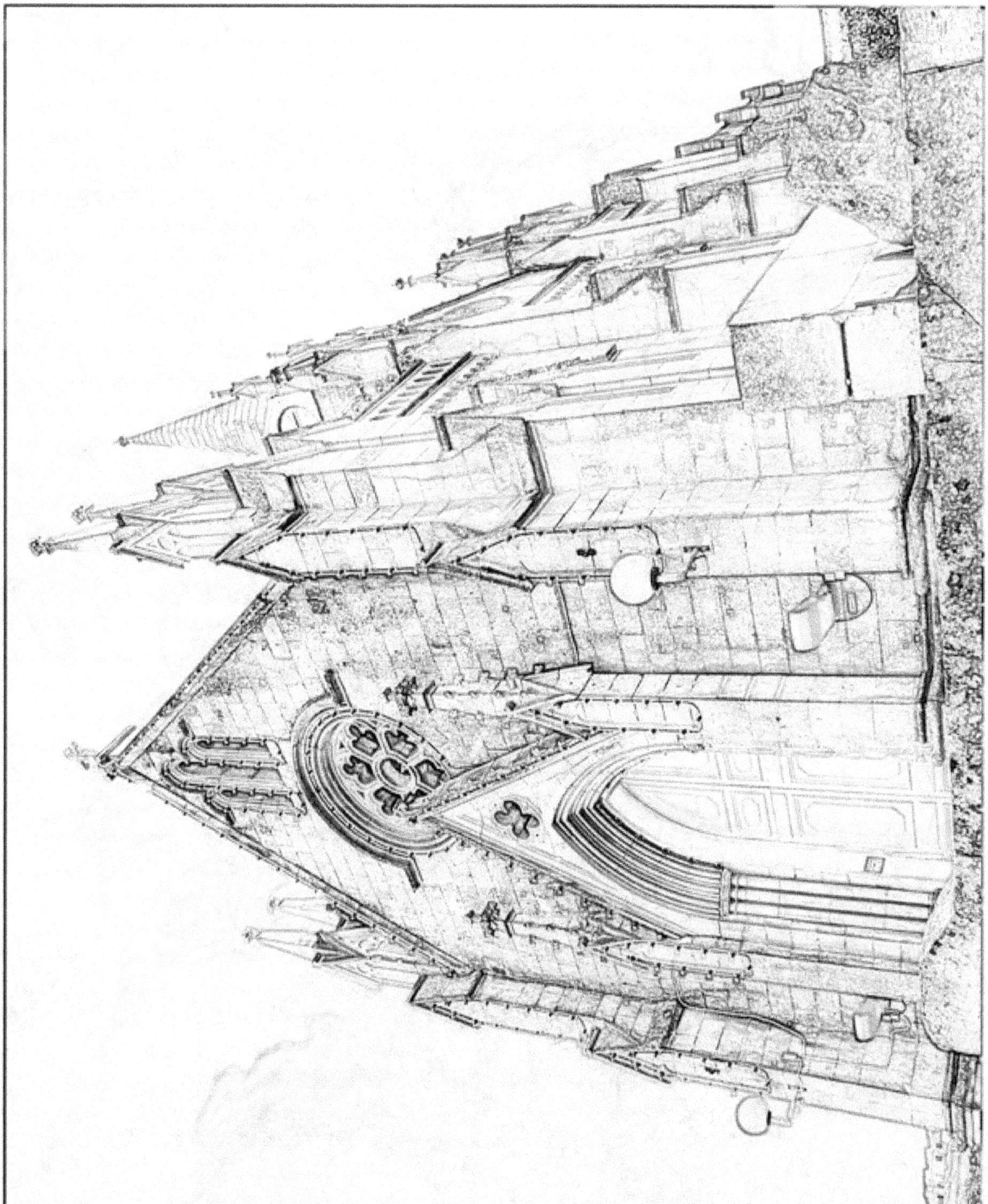

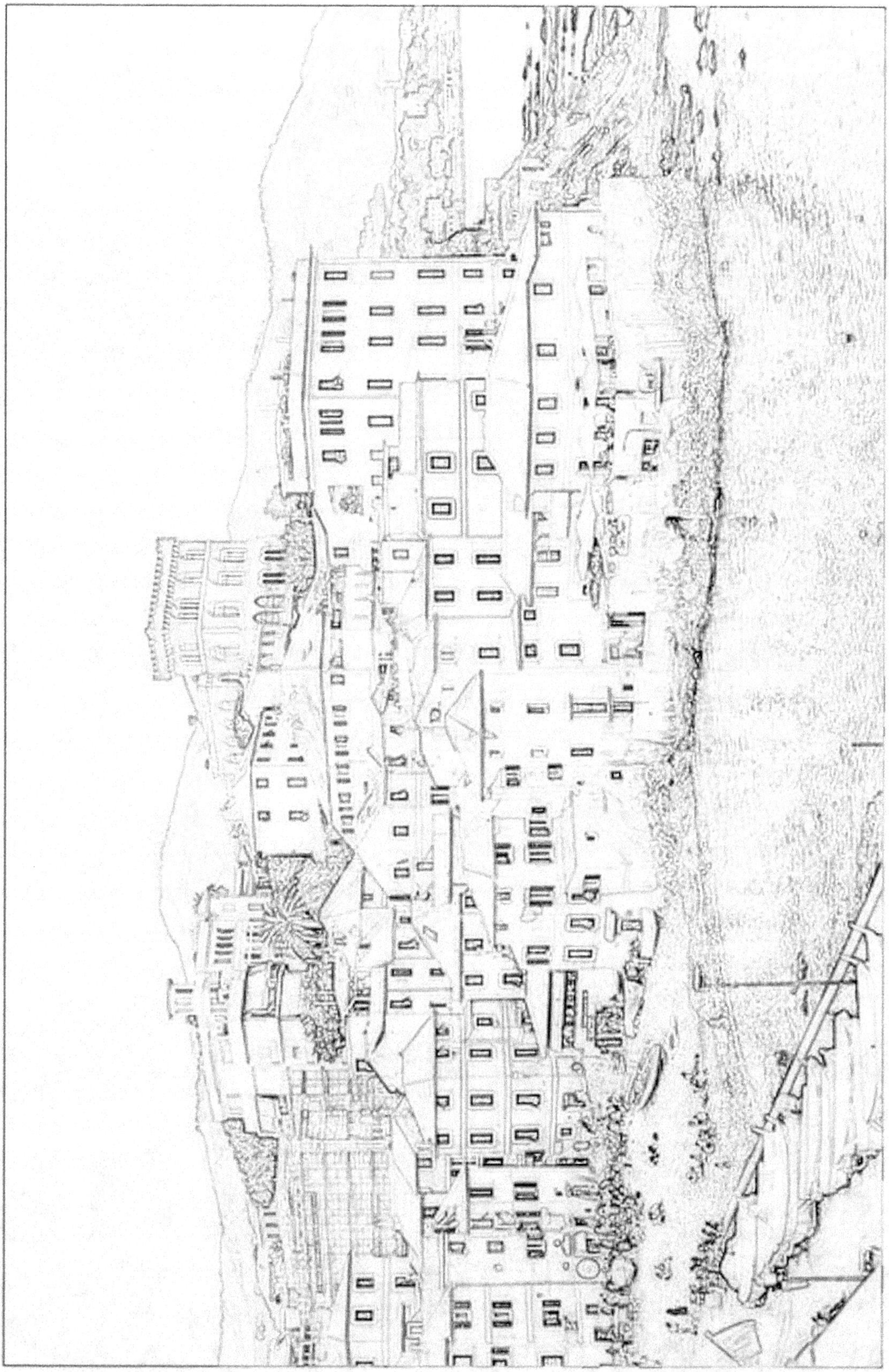

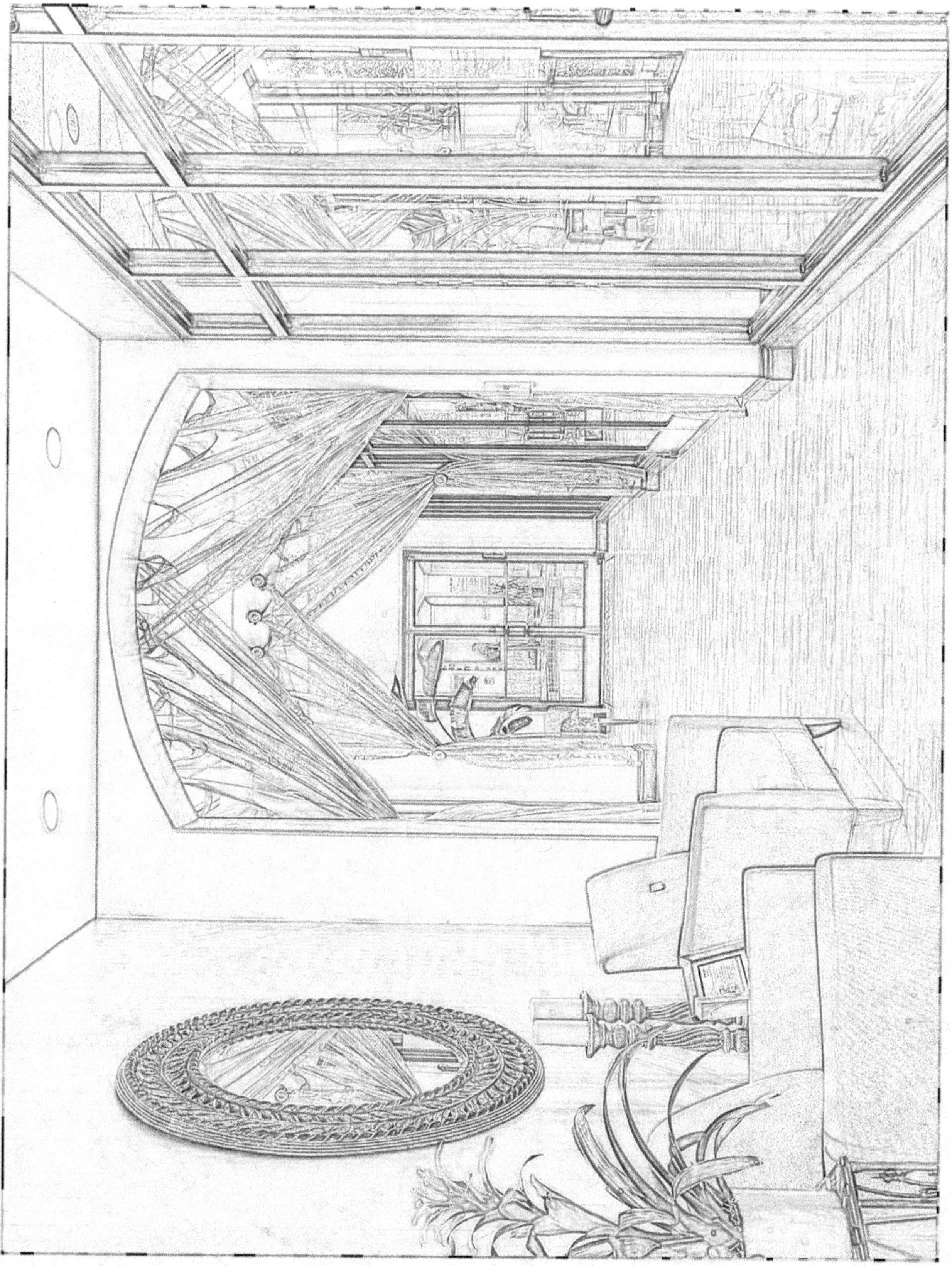

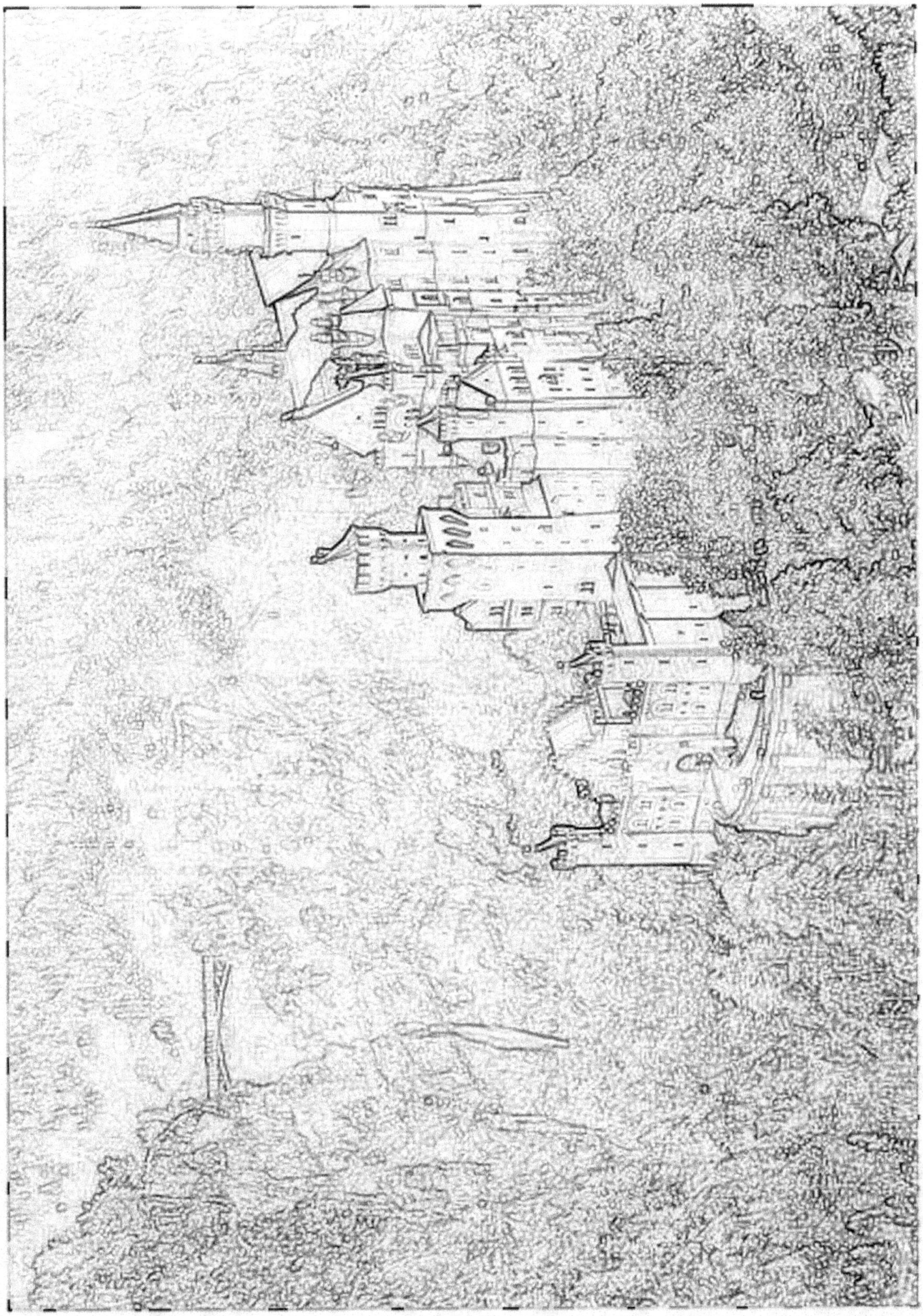

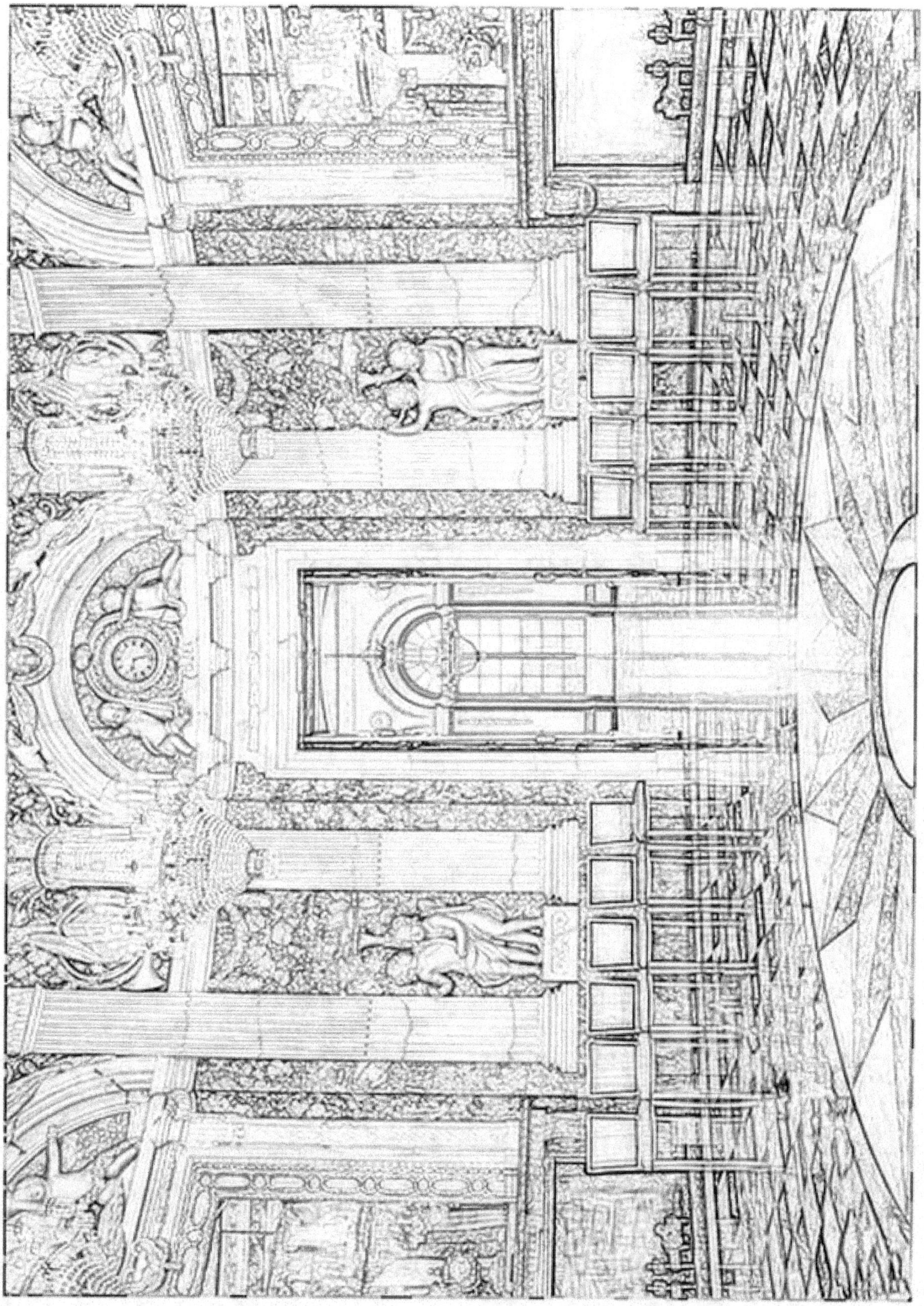

www.ingramcontent.com/pod-product-compliance
Lightning Source LLC
Chambersburg PA
CBHW081736220526
45468CB00008B/2123